PR

The Pursuit of

Happi-Nest

This book needs to be read with a highlighter in one hand. I found myself marking brilliant information on every page. Maybe we should just wallpaper our rooms with MaryJo Bell's pages! You can't stop reading because her warm, wonderful voice makes you feel you've just come to visit a dear friend.

—JONI HILTON, CALIFORNIA (PLAYWRIGHT, THE YOUTUBE MOM, AUTHOR, FORMER TALK SHOW HOST)

No matter where you are in your journey, *The Pursuit of Happi-Nest* will help you. It has helped me. I intend to gift a copy to each of my children—each of whom are thick in the journey of parenting our thirty-one grandchildren. Thank you, MaryJo Bell, for listening and following hints, messages, and lessons from God to bring more love into your own home, and now, blessedly into the lives of—I hope—millions.

—CLAUDETTE BYBEE BURT, IDAHO

MaryJo Bell is a jaunty, charming writer who sprinkles her considerable insights with hard-earned wisdom and delightful stories. She is the friend you wished you could talk to about the challenges of parenting—someone you know you could laugh and cry with and feel better and enlivened for it. You'll wish she lived next door, but traveling with her on the journey in writing to create a loving home is the next-best thing.

—MAURINE PROCTOR, UTAH (COFOUNDER OF *MERIDIAN MAGAZINE*, AUTHOR, AND FORMER JOURNALIST FOR THE *CHICAGO SUN-TIMES*)

Have you ever asked yourself, "Why is it that those Latter-day Saint families seem to like each other so much? How come they seem to raise such awesome, well-adjusted children? Is there some magical key to parenting that I am missing? As a non-Latter-day Saint member, I have often thought someone should come out with an approachable, inspiring book that unlocks some of the shared, foundational principles upon which strong Latter-day Saint families are built. MaryJo Bell's *The Pursuit of Happi-Nest* is that book. From the opening pages, MaryJo draws you in as a friend, engaging your heart with her self-deprecating vulnerability and inspirational testimony. Her forthright observations dispel "perfect family/mom stereotypes" with humor. What emerges is a candid, practical, fast read that will simultaneously keep you chuckling and leave you inspired, motivated and empowered.

—BETSY ROEDER, MARYLAND

MaryJo Bell's book is a treasure trove of exquisitely written stories and quotes that will incentivize your desire to improve the quality of your family life. Her self-deprecating style makes readers feel comfortable, yet she drives home eternally significant values in a courageous manner. The book is compelling and replete with delightful humor. You will want to read it straight through without stopping and give it to all your friends.

—ROBYN ROMNEY EVANS, CALIFORNIA

Funny, insightful, and hard to put down. This is a great book for any parent! Come for the good-hearted, down to earth advice; stay for the hilarious stories.

—EMILY JONES, WASHINGTON

MaryJo Bell is not only a fantastic writer, she is your friend. Her writing style is personable, inspiring, and kind. The stories she shares, and her years of experience are a treasure to all those who read it.

—RACHEL THOMAS, WASHINGTON

The Pursuit of Happi-Nest is heartwarming and hilarious. MaryJo navigates the trenches of motherhood with wisdom while staying relatable. A fun and useful read for any mom.

—KATIE HOLLINGSWORTH, UTAH

In this delightfully engaging book, MaryJo Bell offers profound principles and practices that will fortify your family relationships and beckon heaven into your home. As a mother of eight children, MaryJo's experience authenticates the wisdom she shares with genuine warmth, animated wit and heartfelt love. I am ever grateful for MaryJo's vivacious vision and diligent labor to bring this mothering magnum opus to the masses.

—LAURIE POLLARD, CALIFORNIA

Captured by the title, I picked up this book, and it managed to surpass my expectations. I eagerly read from chapter to chapter. MaryJo's an excellent writer, and her real-life examples bring humility to her advice. I loved the book!

—CAROLE FALTERMEIER, WASHINGTON, PENNSYLVANIA

If you want to help your family battle today's challenges, read this book! It addresses real life concerns with depth, insight, and humor. Filled with delightful stories, it's an easy read, yet it's packed with powerful principles. If you want to make lasting changes in your family, pull up a chair, get comfortable and enjoy!

—LORI JOHNSON, UTAH

Who wouldn't want *more* love at home? In her book, MaryJo provides the perfect blueprint for such a construction project. She teaches her readers about the tools required and how to use them effectively in order to build the happiest possible family and home. She's crafted a masterpiece of parenting wisdom from the heart.

—LESLIE HANSEN, WASHINGTON

MaryJo Bell has created a wonderful book full of practical and inspiring ideas for anyone looking to strengthen home and family. Her wisdom and wit are contagious. A must-read!

—WHITNEY MANNING, VIRGINIA

This book is a must-read for parents wanting to strengthen their homes and families, unify their parenting styles with their spouses, and fortify their children against the temptations that face kids today. The principles in this book are eternal, but they are presented in such a clear and fun way that this book is hard to put down! Pick up a pencil and get ready to take some notes. It will change your life!

—DANA SWARTZ, UTAH

This is an enlightening, inspiring, light-hearted must-read for mothers of all ages. Through MaryJo's honesty about the experiences of life we learn to smile through the tears, pray during the hard times, and look in awe upon the gifts of motherhood.

—THERESA OLIVER, WASHINGTON

This book is a delightful read with useful suggestions interwoven with fun personal anecdotes and real-life examples. I love that the ideas that MaryJo shares are not overwhelming. They can (and should!) be incorporated by everyone.

—TRACY NIELSEN, WASHINGTON

A funny, heartwarming, and relatable look at parenting. A faith-centered approach to parenting that offers greater peace and strength for families.

—KRISTINE NOYES, WASHINGTON

The Pursuit of Happi-Nest is simultaneously warm, affectionate, and educational. It teaches and comforts as it increases your understanding of family. It makes you feel better about your own attempts at parenthood!

—THERESA BELL, UTAH

After reading the book, I recognized that the drive MaryJo had to write it came from her deep love of helping parents. This is especially needed at this time when family traditions and values are being changed by the world. Her experiences, which came from raising not from just two or three kids, but seven and then eight, allowed her to deal with a lot of different kinds of personalities. No matter where you are in raising your family, reading this book will help you get over the humps of parenting. It will also, hopefully, help you to be friends with your kids as they grow into adulthood.

—CARLYN HOOYER, WASHINGTON, THE PHILIPPINES

You will laugh out loud at the wit and want to commit to memory the wisdom of MaryJo Bell's timely self-help manual for parents who want to increase joy in their homes and build life-long positive relationships with their children.

—ANNETTE T., WASHINGTON

MaryJo Bell is a master in the art of gentle inspiration. *The Pursuit of Happi-Nest* is supported by stories that are engaging and heart-warming. Mary's humble confidence in explaining foundational family principles is a showcase of her talent for kind and effective encouragement.

—JARED BELL, TEXAS

MaryJo doesn't just have a gift of making everyone feel loved and important, she really does love everyone and everyone *is* important to her. In *The Pursuit of Happi-Nest*, she tells the genuine stories of parenting in such a way as to validate mamas' experiences, and to delightfully show the delight of being a mama.

—JILL CLEAVER, WASHINGTON

Super fun read but also dives deep into the true foundational FAMILY principles so many people aren't talking about anymore. This book really helped me make changes I had wanted to make for the better in my family life! I laughed, I cried, I couldn't put it down. A must-read for anyone wanting to create a loving, solid family!

—LYNN ROWE, UTAH

The Pursuit of

Happi-Nest

Helping Your Family Soar,
Even While Winging It

Mary Joanne Bell

CFI
An imprint of Cedar Fort, Inc.
Springville, Utah

ISBN 13: 978-1-4621-4187-6

Published by CFI, an imprint of Cedar Fort, Inc.
2373 W. 700 S., Springville, UT 84663
Distributed by Cedar Fort, Inc., www.cedarfort.com

Library of Congress Control Number: 2021950767

Cover design by Shawnda T. Craig
Cover design © 2022 Cedar Fort, Inc.

Printed in the United States of America

10 9 8 7 6 5 4 3 2 1

Printed on acid-free paper

Contents

Preface xi

Introduction 1

Chapter One: Building Family 9

Chapter Two: Building Happi-nest 27

Chapter Three: Building Service Opportunities 41

Chapter Four: Building Virtue 55

Chapter Five: Building Routines 75

Chapter Six: Building Traditions 95

Chapter Seven: Building Ourselves 113

Chapter Eight: Building a Marriage 141

Chapter Nine: Building Vision 161

Chapter Ten: Building Heaven 175

About the Author 187

Remodel Wanted

*Our family is the focus of our greatest work and joy
in this life; so will it be throughout all eternity.*
—*President Russell M. Nelson*[1]

* * *

*All happy families are alike; each unhappy
family is unhappy in its own way.*
—*Leo Tolstoy*[2]

On July 19, 2019, the Holderness family of YouTube fame shared viewers' most searched questions. The first was, "Are you Mormon?" (The Church of Jesus Christ of Latter-day Saints). They are not Latter-day Saints, but this was a natural question because the Holderness family strives to be fun, clean, and family-centered. In other words, Latter-day Saint-ish. The idea of family goes with the Saints like fish and chips, Mickey and Minnie, and salt and pepper. Why do people constantly make an association between strong families and the Latter-day Saints? Why are there so many questions about how Latter-day Saint families build strong families? Where is the book with answers to this? The good news is that right now, you are reading that book.

A number of people have read this manuscript and made comments such as, "I wish I had had this book when my children were very young, or even before I had children." Many of them have asked if they could share this not yet published manuscript with young parents they love. This has been a hard request in some ways. I have wanted to say, "Let's wait until it's published." But I have actually said, "Yes." This is because I have such a heart for young parents. Truthfully, I also wish I had had a book like this when I was in their shoes.

I was always on the lookout for a book written by someone in my situation: a young mom who had "a heart for God" (a phrase my Catholic grandmother used to describe spiritual seekers) but who also felt clueless about how to live up to statements like this one by James E. Faust: "There is no greater good in all the world than motherhood. The influence of a mother in the lives of her children is beyond calculation."[3] Such statements felt intimidating. I wanted an older Latter-day Saint mom (here's looking at you, Titus 2:4–7) to walk me through some practical steps to implement practical Latter-day Saint family-strengthening ideas. I wanted her to explain why these teachings and their applications would make such a difference for my family. In short, I wanted motivation, inspiration, and explanation from a mom who had been in the trenches. Here is that book. It's a little late for me but just in time for those on the current parenting horizon.

You absolutely do not have to be a Latter-day Saint to glean great things from Latter-day Saint principles and practices. Beyond sharing stories, all I have really done in this book is take some of the Latter-day Saint language on family and translate and distill it for the rest of us. You can, of course, tweak this information for your family needs and make it your own.

You are likely reading this because you love your family. This is wonderful. Family relationships offer our greatest potential source for joy in life. Sadly, family can also be the source of our greatest sorrows. The twin goals of this book are to help you avoid family sorrow and increase your family joy.

The metaphor that will be used throughout the book is that of building a home. The goal is to help you build the strongest love-filled home possible.

If you are a Latter-day Saint, I am one of you. If you are not a Latter-day Saint, I am also one of you. For years I was not a Latter-day Saint, and as author Madeline L'Engle has said, "The great thing about getting older is that you don't lose all the other ages you've been."[4] I know what it is to not be Latter-day Saint and be curious about people who seem to be mysteriously known as "Saints." Were they really that good? As it turns out, the Saints are not superhuman, but they are often super at creating humans with solid home lives. I have always been a great believer in solid home and family life, even though for a long time my family of origin life was, well, complicated.

So, before we begin this book on building your stronger home, I would like to introduce myself with a deeply personal story using our building metaphor for this book. We all know how home improvement shows work. They usually begin with a remodeling challenge. Then, a crew sweeps in, does the work, and eventually the master designers are thrilled to see their plans come to fruition.

This story is about my birth family. A lot of heavenly tools and designers were needed to remodel it after it found itself perfectly poised in the arc of a swinging wrecking ball.

Like Nephi, a hero from the Book of Mormon, I too was "born of goodly parents." Good, Catholic parents.

Daddy was our childhood hero. Mom said he looked like the actor Van Johnson, but the six of us kids just thought he was handsome. He smelled like Old Spice, and when he scooped us up in his arms, his tweed coat was always just the right amount of scratchy. I was sure he was a much better dancer than the average daddy, judging by the way he could twirl us around the living room. Although he wasn't a famous singer, he had once considered singing as a career, and that made him famous enough for me.

He was not afraid to sing loudly as we took walks around the neighborhood. We all sang and did not care what the neighbors thought (although we suspected they thought we were pretty talented). It was true that Daddy had to be a boring trial attorney all day. But when he came home, the fun came with him.

Unless Daddy was mad. Mom said Daddy had an Irish temper, meaning he sometimes yelled when we ran out of clean towels, or when we weren't scrambling up to bed fast enough, or when chores weren't done. The yelling could be sudden and startling.

Although we all witnessed his tantrums, I was somehow spared his personal wrath. For the first eighteen years of my life, I cannot remember a harsh conversation between us. We adored each other. We were best friends like Orphan Annie and Daddy Warbucks— only we weren't millionaires, and I wasn't an orphan named Annie. But you get the idea. I was a classic daddy's girl.

Until the third grade, I never worried about losing either of my parents. But that year, one of my former teachers "passed on" (as adults described it). It didn't take long to figure out that people who had passed on were never coming back. This was my first contact with death, and I was determined it would be my last.

The night after the funeral I jumped onto my parents' bed as they lay sleeping. They woke up, groggy and squinting, as I cried, "You can never die! Please, promise me right now that you will never die. Promise that I will never lose you!" My mother promised immediately. My father smiled at me with a puzzled look. There was a dim sparkle in his eyes, which I took as a yes and bounced back up to bed, reassured that we were all safe from change.

But change came. As I made my way through high school, Dad's hair got grayer and mine morphed into Farrah Fawcett layers. My best friend was Dana Rowe, the most honest person I had ever known. She was open with me about her beliefs, and I found myself intrigued by her Latter-day Saint religion. That's when things got complicated.

One day, Dana and I were engaged in our favorite pastime: chatting and laughing with occasional swearing. Actually, I was the one doing all the swearing. Dana's sister was home from college, and she looked at me with gentleness. Pressing her finger to her lips she said softly, "Shh."

Something happened then that would change me forever. Something ran through me with a quick, powerful intensity that felt like painless electricity. For just a moment, it literally took my breath away, and I was left knowing something unequivocally, something I had not known before: God did not want me to swear. I didn't say anything, but instantly I swore off swearing.

One Sunday, Dana invited me to visit her church. We arrived early. The building was clean and tastefully decorated. Families were dressed in their Sunday best. There was a spirit of animated camaraderie as they all mingled together.

Dana introduced me to a gentle, petite woman with dark brown hair. She did not seem to recognize me, although I was sure we had met somewhere before. I just couldn't place where it was, or when. Then Dana introduced me to someone else, and I experienced a similar déjà vu moment. To my wonderment, this experience kept repeating itself with each introduction. Finally, I stood in the back of the chapel, surveying the little social knots of people that had formed before the services began. Tears formed in my eyes as it slowly dawned on me that I knew them all. Deep in my soul, I knew that somewhere, at some time, these people had once been my close friends. There was a great feeling of belonging coupled with an unexpected feeling of relief. I kept thinking, "I am home."

We sat down, and the service began. Watching reverent teenage boys in white shirts and ties (a rare sight) pass the sacrament was beautiful. Then five little girls in white, all sisters, sang "Love at Home." It was a simple song, but its message was profound. Something seemed to echo from eternity: the family unit was sacred, divine, and of critical importance to the Lord. Someone spoke of forever families sealed together in the temples of the Lord. I couldn't remember hearing anything like that before, and yet the sudden realization of its truth was so touching it brought tears to my eyes.

Until that morning, I thought I understood the purpose of church. It was a place for individuals to commune and celebrate their individual relationships with a higher power. I was genuinely surprised to learn that God was interested in so much more than just the individual. He wanted the whole family. His plan for family bonding and joy was, apparently, specific and organized. He was not messing around with vagaries. There was work to be done all right, and His church—if it was His church—was apparently not afraid of the hard work it took to bind families together.

My soul suddenly yearned for these blessings for my mother and father, my brothers and sisters. We were a good family, but through the Spirit that day I could sense that so much more was possible. God wanted to bring us to heaven together: pure, whole, and forever.

I left in a quiet, contemplative state, but my busy high school life soon got the best of me. The Spirit that had been present at church did not stay with me, and I locked the experience away in a place in my heart labeled "Marvel About This Again . . . Someday."

A few weeks later Dana gave me a pamphlet on Joseph Smith, which I tucked inside one of my textbooks. That night, as I tossed my books on my bed, the pamphlet fell out. I picked it up with curiosity. I read Joseph's account again and again, searching for subtle clues signaling dishonesty. I couldn't find them. Joseph's voice was so pure and without guile that it touched me to the core. In the deepest part of my soul, I wrestled with the question: Had Jesus and Heavenly Father appeared to Joseph Smith in the spring of 1820? The thought was stunning, joyful, petrifying.

What if I learned it was all true? My family would never accept a new faith; we had been Catholic for centuries. It was hard not to think of the third daughter in *Fiddler on the Roof* who had a change of faith and ended up cut off from her family forever. The thought of breaking up with my family terrified me.

Over the next two years, I tried to study the restored gospel of Jesus Christ from all angles. As it turned out, there were a lot of angles, but I had to be sure. I spent a year at Brigham Young University and another year at St. Mary's of Notre Dame. I took religion classes and talked to Catholic priests. I talked to members of other faiths. I talked to members of Dana's church and felt that same electricity run through me as when they had borne their testimonies. But mostly, I talked to God.

I felt He wanted me to prayerfully study the Book of Mormon, the Doctrine and Covenants, and the Pearl of Great Price. I put off the idea for a long time. Finally, at nineteen, I read the Book of Mormon with a prayer in my heart, and just knew.

I had already had so many spiritual experiences by then, so many witnesses of the truth, but the answer I received of the Book of Mormon's truthfulness was solid. It was too hard to deny. So much of me didn't want to know what I knew, and I felt empathy for Joseph Smith's statement: "I knew it, and I knew God knew it, and I could not deny it" (Joseph Smith—History 1:25). I was nineteen.

Now it was "all over but the shoutin'." I had a feeling that Dad would take care of that.

The night before my baptism I was terrified. Alone in my room, I poured out my heart to God. Why did He want me to do this? Why was it so impossible? I knew Dad would be angry and wouldn't understand. I knew his love for me might change. I had relied on that love for so long. I wasn't sure I could live without it.

I tried to recall the first time I went to church with Dana and the powerful feelings I had there about family. From the beginning, I had known deeply that this faith had the power to bless families like no other. It could bless my parents, my siblings, my future family. I knew by the Spirit that this was what God had in mind: blessing my family. Somehow, I knew—I just absolutely knew—that all of the current mess would eventually bless us all. A fortress of strength would one day replace what was about to be destroyed. But that was someday.

I pushed my head into my pillow and sobbed. I knew God understood. I could feel His compassion. That alone made me want to weep. But there were other good reasons to cry. I sensed that things were going to get a lot worse before they got better. I just didn't know how much worse.

After my baptism, Dad insisted that I leave home permanently. All financial help, which had previously been generous, was cut off. A couple of jobs and an academic scholarship helped me return to BYU, but Dad initially insisted that even my mother and siblings have little to do with me.

The loving father I had known packed up his laughter and kindness and left. A vacant look replaced the sparkle in his eyes as emotional amnesia took hold of him. He no longer seemed to recognize me as his daughter.

A decade of near silence followed, occasionally punctuated by fury. Sometimes he would throw me an anti-Mormon question, never intending to let me answer. There was no way to compete with his trial lawyer tenacity, his filibuster acumen. It was like talking into a wind tunnel; the cacophony of his resistance was so intense that all meaning was lost.

I gave up. I refused to respond in anger when no family members attended my wedding reception. I did not comment when my husband patiently listened to my father's religious opinions for hours at a time.

But my good husband always made sure we never stopped praying for Dad. Early in our marriage, especially, we prayed morning and night that whatever stood between Dad and the gospel would fall away.

One of my relatively few conversations with Dad took place about two years after I married. Mom told me Dad was about to call, and I stared as the phone rang. This was going to be significant. "God spoke to me, Mary," he said. "He spoke to me out loud. He told me that I would never drink again, and that I would never have a desire to drink again."

I was speechless.

Years later Mom told me that Dad's temper issues had always been deeply connected to drinking alcohol. I was shocked. I had never seen Dad drink heavily. I had never known about this struggle. She said Dad's experience with God launched the best years of their marriage; the start of twenty-four years (and counting) without alcohol. Dad said he never desired it after that day he heard God's voice.

About twenty-five years after my baptism, I had a prompting to organize a formal reunion for Dad's side of the family. This ranked near the top of my list of good things I did not want to do. We came, we rented, we catered; it all went pretty smoothly.

At the end, Dad was full of compliments. He said my mother looked gorgeous, my sister sang like an opera star, my siblings and cousins couldn't possibly be more marvelous. Then Dad nodded cordially in my direction, bowed formally, and left.

The next night my family, together with a couple of siblings and their children, had a family home evening. Miraculously, Dad came. The warmth of the Spirit settled around us, bringing us close and thawing my frozen heart.

Later, when nearly everyone left for ice cream, Dad and I wound up in the quiet living room. I recall our conversation this way.

"Dad, can I talk to you about something?" I asked.

"Yes, what is it?"

I took a deep breath.

"I just wanted to tell you that all of the reunion stuff . . . a lot of that was for you." I smiled nervously. "I just wanted you to know that I love you." Annoyed by tears forming in my eyes, I brushed them away. But Dad's eyes were narrowed in concentration. He wanted to hear more. I took another breath and continued.

"So, I . . . I just wanted you to know that it's been really hard, I mean all these years. Anyway, I hoped the reunion would please you. It has always been my hope that I would please you. Do you remember when I was a little girl and I would perform in front of an audience sometimes? Well, I just wanted you to know that it was actually you that I was scanning the audience for. It was always your approval, your validation, that meant the most to me. Do you remember how I would defend you when your temper would get the best of you and others would criticize you? I always took your side because . . . because I believed in you, Dad."

I could hear my voice getting softer. I looked right at him and reached out for his hand. I took another deep breath and sent up a silent prayer for courage. "I only joined the Church because God told me to. I never did it to offend you. I would never want to do anything to hurt you. Please believe me." I took another deep breath. "I believe the Church is true."

The Spirit was nearly palpable. Neither of us spoke for a long time. The dishwasher hummed quietly in the kitchen.

Dad cleared his throat. His posture was soldier straight as he spoke in even, measured words. "The worst thing I have ever done"—Dad paused to compose himself—"is what I did to you. For this . . . I am truly sorry." Tears glistened in his eyes. His shoulders trembled slightly.

"It's okay," I said, patting his shoulder, tears hurrying down my cheeks. "I love you. Thank you for listening to me." *Thank you for recognizing me*, I thought. I couldn't stop crying. Our carefully maintained walls of pride were crumbling.

We heard footsteps shuffling toward the front door and gentle laughter. I looked out the window. There were my children and husband, my lanky six-foot-four college student son carrying my diminutive five-year-old, her soft brown hair blowing behind her in the summer wind. My husband was dipping his head down to listen to another of our daughters. I recognized the look of adoration in her eyes.

I squeezed Dad's hand. What were a few decades between friends? It didn't matter. It couldn't matter. Forever was ahead of us. I threw my arms around his neck and hugged him like I was five.

Things got better and better from there. In the last chapter of this book, I will share with you the end of this story. In the meantime, know that the Master Designers in heaven had certainly been watching over us and answering prayers. Using some of the tools we will discuss in the next chapters, they taught us how to rebuild our family relationships. They did the heavy lifting.

NOTES

1. Russell M. Nelson, "Set in Order Thy House," *Ensign or Liahona*, November 2001, 69.
2. Tolstoy, Leo. "Anna Karenina, by Leo Tolstoy - Project Gutenburg," May 22, 2020. https://www.gutenberg.org/files/1399/1399-h/1399-h.htm.
3. James E. Faust, "Fathers, Mothers, Marriage," *Ensign*, August 2004; https://www.churchofjesuschrist.org/study/liahona/2004/08/fathers-mothers-marriage?lang=eng.
4. Madeleine L'Engle, "Author to Readers," *The New York Times*, April 25, 1985; https://www.nytimes.com/1985/04/25/nyregion/new-york-day-by-day-author-to-readers.html.

Introduction

The most important work you will ever do will be within the walls of your own home.
—Harold B. Lee [1]

Hello, friend! Is it okay if I call you friend? In my early twenties I worked in a bank, and sometimes a son of then Latter-day Saint prophet Ezra Taft Benson would come in to do typical banking things. He would look at all of us slightly bored bank tellers, wave, and say, "Hello, friends!" I didn't know him, but he thought of me as a friend. I was surprised and glad at the same time. Similarly, you and I may not have met in this life, but, hey, we can be friends. I mean, we were friends back in heaven, right? We're getting ahead of ourselves, though. Let's start at the beginning.

How are you? We aren't having lunch right now, with you answering that question, of course. Still, I hope you are well. I hope you are somewhere comfy. Maybe you are at home in jammies or sweats and you have a little something delicious to sip or munch. I hope you are enjoying some rest time just for you. You deserve it.

This book was written to help you "family." Wherever you are in your family building experience, even if you have yet to build your own family, this is all for you. If you are a grandparent, welcome! I am too. There is a lot of content that applies equally to grandchildren. If you are a mother with young children, you have an extra special place in my "been there" heart. When I see families with little children, I have to resist the urge to give them hugs. You are doing the job that Oprah described as "the toughest"[2] and C.S. Lewis described as "the most important," the one "for which all other jobs exist."[3]

To quote a line from the musical *Gigi*, "Ah yes, I remember it well." There was so much joy then, but sometimes it felt like CHAOS (Can't Have Anyone Over Syndrome).[4] You may feel overwhelmed sometimes. I get it.

I remember a day when our oldest was nine with four younger siblings. I had a super busy husband. I lived 3,000 miles away from my family of origin. I had grown up with a full-time housekeeper in our Maryland home. Now I was on my own, in so many ways. Although I had been the fortunate beneficiary of an outstanding college education, I often felt totally baffled by all that my current life demanded. Can you relate to parental overwhelm?

On this day our son had a school Halloween party he wanted me to attend. All the parents had been invited. I got him out the door for school and told him I would meet him at the class party later that day. I prepped the treat I was supposed to bring. I got everyone bathed, fed, and into their Halloween costumes. I tried to get everyone to the car. Then the baby wanted to nurse again, the toddlers couldn't find their shoes, one child didn't want to go . . . you know the drill. By the time we got there we were quite late. The party was almost over. We pulled up in front of the school, and I rushed to get everyone out of car seats and back into costumes they had removed on the way to school.

When I walked into the classroom I was flustered and out of breath, and the wind had blown much of my hair into my eyes. I looked like a beleaguered Havanese dog. Because we were so late, the whole classroom turned toward us as we entered. One older woman looked directly at me and said with a slow smile, "God loves you, Mary." Tears sprung to my eyes. Did God love me? Did He see how hard I was trying and how unsuccessful I felt sometimes? Did He see how hard this job of mothering was? Also, did He see how nice this woman was? Had He inspired her to say that? If your answer is a nod of possible agreement, we are on the same page. (Actually, we are also on the same actual page as we are both reading this. Ha ha! I'm glad we're friends.)

Would you like more peace in your home? Would you like to strengthen your family? Have you ever felt that dark forces were conspiring against your efforts to build a stronger and more loving home? This is because *dark forces are conspiring against your efforts to build a stronger and more loving home.* Hello, life! We signed up for this mortal experience knowing there would be adversity and challenges, and knowing that these things could make us stronger and better over time.

As parents, our mutual goal is to partner with our Creator to build, remodel, and maintain a home so emotionally and spiritually strong that even the metaphorical "wolf at the door" will not be able to knock it down.

The fact that you are reading a book right now on fortifying families indicates great things about you. You care about families. You care about children. You care about goodness. You are humble and want to learn. I applaud you.

Perhaps there is no better time for a book on learning to be comfortable, peaceful, and happier at home. Home, of course, is where our hearts have been all along.

Deeply wise, Mother Teresa once said, "If you want to change the world, go home and love your family."[5] Mother Teresa knew that the most valuable "product" any society produces is its next generation of families. After all, the family is the most fundamental unit of society. Healthy, happy families are the building blocks of a healthy, happy civilization.

The desire for a happy home is universal and spans all human history. You never hear someone say to a therapist, "You gotta help me, Doc. I had such a functional, peaceful childhood. I don't know how to recover." The reality is that therapists' offices are stuffed with people trying to untangle chaotic, broken, even violent childhoods. On a global scale, families are in a downward spiral.[6]

The decades since 1960 tell a sad story: In 1960, 73 percent of children lived in a home with two married parents in their first marriage. Today that number is 46 percent. In 1960, 5 percent of children were born outside of marriage. Today that number is 41 percent. In addition, single parenthood has tripled since 1960.[7]

Somewhere along the line, humans got distracted from the primary goal of life's missions: to create and maintain loving families. But by every possible measure (economic, emotional, community stability, and so on) the world depends on strong families.

"Who," we may silently call out to the universe, "can help us save the family institution? Who can help us raise healthy families in a world that doesn't always feel healthy for families?"

Could it be Latter-day Saints? Yes. I realized this as a young adult convert to The Church of Jesus Christ of Latter-day Saints. I noticed that in today's unpredictable, often chaotic world, many were struck by the outstanding and consistent Latter-day Saint witness to successful family life. "What is it about Latter-day Saints?" people have often asked me. "Why do their families often seem so happy and well adjusted? Is there some magical reason their kids often turn out so well? Seriously, fill me in. What am I missing here?" You too may have thought, "Why not investigate a model for happy family life that *is working well?*"

If you are not a member of The Church of Jesus Christ of Latter-day Saints, you aren't necessarily asking this question because you want to become a Latter-day Saint. You may just want some ideas you can adapt to fit into your own family. Or, you may be a new member of the Church looking for "up close and personal" Latter-day Saint family experiences. Or possibly, you grew up in or around the Latter-day Saint faith, but you are seeking more information as you raise your own children. You might be a curious parent or grandparent of any faith, or no faith at all. To all of these groups and more, welcome to this book. There is laughter and learning ahead for all of us.

Whatever one's belief system or unique life experience, we all aspire to raise joyful, well-adjusted kids and foster healthy, loving interactions with the people around us. Although there is no perfect home on earth, there are proven, proactive Latter-day Saint strategies that can help families.

Many people hear the term "Mormon*" or "LDS" and think of well-known families such as the Osmonds; the Romneys; the Marriotts; business leader Stephen R. Covey; former politicians Jeff Flake or Harry Reid; the King Family Singers; Tina Cole from the 1960s sitcom *My Three Sons* (who was also a member of the King family); musicians Gladys Knight, David Archuletta, Brooke White, and Brandon Flowers; snowboarder Torah Bright; filmmaker (*Napoleon Dynamite*) Jared Hess; actor Jon Heder; and politicians Harry Reid and Orrin Hatch. These are good people, but the Latter-day Saint track record for building peaceful, happy families also includes millions of less visible Saints. They all live by principles and ideas you can also access. These statistics are telling:

- *Psychology Today* recently estimated that married couples sealed in Latter-day Saint temples have a divorce rate of about 10 percent.[8]
- Brigham Young University in Provo, Utah, was voted the number-one graduate school for Marriage and Family Studies in 2016.[9]
- Year in and year out, Utah ranks as the happiest, or one of the happiest, states in the country.[10]

Of course, the Saints experience heartbreaking challenges common to mankind. But they have a toolbox filled with excellent tools, and they know how to use them. They build. When things fall apart, they rebuild, relying on God, the Master builder. You can use these tools too. You will learn about many of them in the following chapters.

Our own family has experienced rebuilding periods. Sometimes projects have seemed overwhelming and even completely impossible. My story in the preface is one example of this. Sometimes the

---

* (Members of The Church of Jesus Christ of Latter-day Saints are often known as Mormons. However, they are no longer called "Mormons" and prefer to be called "Latter-day Saints" (or sometimes just Saints for short.) The Church is now exclusively called by its original name, The Church of Jesus Christ of Latter-day Saints.)

reconstruction jobs are smaller. For example, our oldest son became physically ill partway through his two-year church mission and had to come home early. He returned to the field seven years later. His younger brother by nine years got the same illness on his mission. Then, a daughter became seriously ill on her mission to the Philippines! These were rough seas we had to sail, but blue skies were eventually on the horizon. All three are totally healthy now, and we pray they will always enjoy good health. Our oldest son, inspired by what he learned about health through his ordeal, is now a naturopathic physician.

It all works out in the end. If it hasn't worked out, as they say, "It's not the end yet!" The end may not happen until after we pass through the veil and are back home in heaven. Mortality is often "the messy middle." Whatever we may suffer here isn't forever. Time really does heal all wounds. The next life will be a place where many concerns we have about our children, family relationships, and so on are at last resolved. We believe that God has His watchful eye on all of His children. They are His children too. He does "work in mysterious ways."** He knows exactly what He is doing. We just need to try to set good examples and love with all of our hearts. Time is forever on our side.

I once read about a man who had a near-death experience. At the time he was an atheist and was living a life of poor choices. He said that he saw Christ in this experience and was surprised and expectant of what he felt would be a deserved chastisement. But the Savior only looked at him with oceans of love in His eyes. The Savior simply asked, "What did you learn?"

** You can learn more about strengthening families on my family's new podcast, *Moms Meet World*. It is streaming on all major, and most minor, platforms. Additionally, you can read my monthly column in *Meridian Magazine* at online.https://latterdaysaintmag.com/following-the-prophets-example-in-dealing-with-contention/.

As a side note, if you are not familiar with the teachings of The Church of Jesus Christ of Latter-day Saints, you may have some questions. If you have a Latter-day Saint friend, you could ask them, of course. Another option is to contact a Latter-day Saint missionary. They love questions! Go to comeuntochrist.org/requests/missionary-visit.

We're all just here to learn. Learning takes time. When we add eternity to the mix, we have all the time we and our families need.

The Pursuit of Happi-Nest is sprinkled with the Latter-day Saint perspective, but many of the concepts are in harmony with those of other faiths, or with those of no particular faith at all. This book is comprised of ten chapters, each chapter contributing a design element to the stronger homes we are striving to build. At the end of most chapters there is a "Nuts & Bolts" section where you will find summaries and/or additional ideas.

President Russell M. Nelson, prophet and president of The Church of Jesus Christ of Latter-day Saints, recently said, "I invite you . . . to create a home that is a place of security."[11]

Let's build those places of security. Let's turn on all the lights.

NOTES

1. Harold B. Lee, *Teachings of Presidents of the Church: Harold B. Lee* (2000), 134.

2. Eleanor Barkhorn, "'There's No Tougher Job than Being a Mom'," *The Atlantic*. Atlantic Media Company, July 11, 2013; https://www.theatlantic.com/sexes/archive/2013/07/theres-no-tougher-job-than-being-a-mom/277685/.

3. C. S. Lewis, *Yours, Jack: Spiritual Direction from C.S. Lewis.* Edited by Paul F. Ford (New York, NY: Harper One, 2008), 260.

4. "Can't Have Anyone Over Syndrome" see Peggy Jones and Pam Young, *Sidetracked Home Executives* (1981).

5. The actual author of this quote is unknown, but it has been incorrectly attributed to Mother Teresa.

6. Internationally recognized expert on global trends, Chapman University Professor Joel Kotkin has written, "In the coming decades, success will accrue to those cultures that preserve the family's place." He has also said that the preservation of the family "is the civilizational issue of our time." He asks, "Is the family at the center of society, or is it not? If you take the family out of the societal equation you begin to get all kinds of dysfunction. We're already seeing it. I don't see how civilization as we know it will continue if we continue in the direction we are going. We are headed into a very dangerous place" (Joel Kotkin and Harry Siegel, "Is the Family Finished?" *The Daily Beast*, February 21, 2013; https://joelkotkin.com/00702-family-finished/).

7. Gretchen Livingston, "Fewer than Half of Us Kids Live in 'Traditional' Family." Pew Research Center, May 30, 2020. https://pewresearch.org/fact-tank/2014/12/22/ less-than-half-of-u-s-kids-today-live-in-a-traditional-family/.

8. Carrie A. Moore, "Statistics Offer Good and Bad News for LDS," *Deseret News*, August 11, 2002; https://www.deseret.com/2002/8/11/19671265/ statistics-offer-good-and-bad-news-for-lds.

9. Madison Everett, "BYU's Marriage and Family Therapy Program Named No. 1 in Nation," *The Daily Universe*, Brigham Young University, March 7, 2019; https://universe.byu.edu/2019/03/06/ byus-marriage-and-family-therapy-program-named-no-1-in-nation/.

10. Adam McCann, "Happiest States in America," *WalletHub*, September 14, 2021. https://wallethub.com/edu/happiest-states/6959.

11. Russell M. Nelson, "Embrace the Future with Faith," *Ensign or Liahona*, November 2020, 73.

Chapter One
Building Family

Family is not an important thing.
It's everything.[1]
—Michael J. Fox

* * *

A soft answer turneth away wrath.
—Proverbs 15:1

Love for our families is the cement that holds our family relationships together. When I have asked young parents what they want most, the answers are often similar: to be more patient; to have a calmer home; to be able to handle chaos without losing it. The good news is that you are about to receive more serenity. You can use it to build your stronger home and family. Hold my virtual hand. Let's go!

Patience is the number-one parenting tool. Patience is the BMW, the Gucci bag, and the latest iPhone of parenting. We're all craving calm. We want the home to be a refuge of safety and peace. (Is there any other place left?) We know if we can "keep our heads when others are losing theirs and blaming it on us," family peace will increase.

Mothers set the tone. You know the saying: "When Momma's not happy ain't nobody happy." Whether rarely home or always home or somewhere in-between, the mother is the heart of her home. Sometimes she feels like the liver of the home, filtering societal toxins. Or she may feel like the pancreas of the home, trying to deal with all the sticky, sugary stuff trying to enter. But usually, she's the heart. And she's aware of the heart of everyone who lives there.

Similarly, a father can anchor the home like nothing else. He can help his family feel grounded, stable, and safe. I love it when my husband works at home, even if he is crazy busy and we can hardly talk.

An enormous piece of the peace puzzle is resisting the temptation to yell. I want to yell it from the rooftops: "Not yelling changes everything!" The resultant calmer feeling in your home will help cement your relationships with trust. Your home will be noticeably stronger. To your children, it will feel safer. It will be a place where all can truly relax.

NOT YELLING 101

We all know the feeling. We are frustrated about something, and as our frustration increases, so does the temptation to dial up the volume of our voices. But we may also know this (framable) quote by Latter-day Saint prophet David O. McKay: "There should be no yelling in the home unless there is a fire."[3] So then, we have to light something on fire. I'm kidding! But the situation can be challenging, especially when it comes to parenting.

If new parents could choose any attribute to instantly have, isn't there a good chance they would choose patience? This would have been my choice. It seems that what we parents want most is serenity . . . now!

Truly, family life can feel joy-fueled and wonder-filled. It can be "Kodak moments" and Kleenex. It can be "running through fields of daisies holding the hands of those we love." But then suddenly, seemingly out of nowhere, it can feel that we have tripped and somersaulted into the Grand Canyon of Annoyance. We may be tempted to raise our voices.

We don't want to raise our voices. We really, *really* don't want to raise our voices. But it's hard because children can be immature and demanding and—oh my goodness what is this sudden, massive mess, and where are the 800 socks I bought you, and please just Get. In. The. Car! And we are not yelling because we don't want to break their beautiful spirits that just arrived from heaven. God entrusted them to us! We want to set good examples for them so that they won't yell, so that they can reach their full potential more easily, so that they can be happier, so that they can grow up and teach their children not to yell so that they can be happier, so that there can be more peace on earth or whatever. And why is there so much pressure on parents, and why do we feel like yelling about this?

My husband and I didn't want to yell at our children or at each other because we knew that yelling brought contention and we believed in this: "He that hath the spirit of contention is not of me but is of the devil, who is the father of contention, and he stirreth up the hearts of men to contend with anger, one with another" (3 Nephi 11:29).

Fortunately, patience is an invisible 'muscle' that can be developed, like any other muscle. It takes time, practice, and self-forgiveness.

Getting to calm(er) did not happen for me overnight. Or over a fortnight. Or in a fort. At night. First, I made a firm choice to try not to ever raise my voice. Then it was trial and effort. It was a trial to put in so much effort. So, I began to rely on what may be a surprising game changer: prayer. I just started praying for patience and a heart of love everywhere and anytime. Often, I was on my desperate knees.

One day a man knocked on our door and our three-year-old, Emily, answered it.

"Hello," the man said. "Is your mommy home?"

"Oh . . . she's home. But she can't come to the door right now."

"Why not?"

11

"Because she's in there." Emily pointed to another room.

"What is she doing?"

"Umm . . . she's kneeling down. She's praying that she won't yell at us!"

I wanted a contention/yell-free environment because my husband and I also believed in these words by Harold B. Lee: "When you raise your voice in anger, the Spirit departs from your home." We didn't want to chase that beautiful gift, the Spirit, away.

Prayer can even work when people aren't sure they believe in God. An agnostic friend told me:

> I wasn't totally sure if there was a God. But I would "pray"—literally beg—when the kids were nuts. I would pray the same thing over and over: "Please help me not to yell. Please. I don't want to yell. Please help me. Just, please." I would just keep on with this prayer, or whatever it was, until at last I would feel the anger that had been rising in my chest start to subside. I had never really wanted to yell, but I just felt so helpless and didn't know what else to do. To my surprise, the prayer thing changed things. That's when I started thinking, this is science. Every time I do this, things get better.

I can second her emotions. I've been tempted to yell countless times, but as I have prayed, the frenzy in my heart would abate. Prayer can work miracles. It can help us to be gentle with everyone. It helps us use our personal power for good. Love can increase, crowding out resentment.

And when we stay calmer in our homes, there is a ripple effect that goes out into the world. As a nation, we could use some serious calm, couldn't we? We want our homes to be places of refuge, safety, and peace.

We know the key maneuver for dodging contention: "A soft answer turneth away wrath, but grievous words stir up anger" (Proverbs 15:1). Softness for the win. We may not get peace on (all of the) earth right away, but we can get more peace in our homes right away, as we keep in mind the mighty power of our soft response.

One day a woman I barely knew approached me with a suspicious look in her eye. "Do you know Diane?" she asked. "She's a Latter-day Saint."

"Yes! I love Diane," I said.

"Yes," she continued, raising her eyebrows. "I was pretty sure you did. She's not a yeller, you know." She looked me over. "You're not either. I can just tell. You're one of those . . . you know, those . . . non-yelling people. But some of us aren't like that, you know. We yell. That's just how we do our parenting. It works for us!"

Huh?

Yelling can *seem* like it's working. Especially in the short term. But what about the longer term? Children are like behavioral boomerangs. Behaviors come back to us. We don't want our children to yell at us. This was a big reason I worked hard on "tranquilit-me."

I decided to try not to raise my voice in early motherhood. But at first, it was trial and error. It was a trial, making all those errors.

One day when our three oldest children were very young, I wrote in my journal, "Spent the day yelling, 'Stop yelling!'" I put the journal down and thought, *Yelling can* seem *like it's working. Especially in the short term. But what about the longer term?*

The truth is that yelling lies. Yelling may get kids to behave in the short term, but it may have long-term consequences. It invites the spirit of contention into our homes. Yelling may teach children to yell at us and at each other. It may teach children to yell at themselves internally.

On the other hand, "staying gentle" ("Be gentle," we remind toddlers) invites a spirit of peace and love into our homes. Once in a while, I still whisper, "Be gentle," to teens when they forget to frame frustration with good manners.

NOT YELLING 200

Now let's go a little deeper. What could be at the roots of our inclinations to yell?

Could those roots be connected to a challenging child(ren)? What if a particular child seems to consistently drive us to the breaking point? What if a different child was equally difficult in the same way, but we weren't as ruffled by the behavior? If you've been there, I've also done that. I didn't understand what was happening at a subconscious level.

Let me explain. You've noticed that we can give birth to a child that reminds us of someone from our family of origin. Maybe your son looks a lot like your dad. Maybe your daughter can sing like your Aunt Jane. This is all great, right?

But what if this son or daughter reminds you a lot of someone from your family of origin with whom you have struggled in the past? At least subconsciously, you may have to struggle again, as you interact with this new person who reminds you of the "old" person from your past. So many humans, including myself, have been in this emotional wind-tossed boat.

We don't always make the connection between past emotional baggage and current parenting. We may feel confused. But we want to figure it out because if we don't, that confusion can cue the dance of dysfunction. Music, maestro, misery.

For example, you've read far enough to know about my dad's temper. When we had our first son, who was delightful and gregarious like my dad, I also secretly feared that he might have my dad's temper tendencies. My stomach was in knots over this. In an effort to make sure he didn't grow up with a temper, at first I gave him more than necessary time-outs concerning being respectful. When I understood the irrational connection I was making between my fear and my father, I was finally able to relax, reconsider, and relate more compassionately with our son.

Another time, I gave birth to a daughter. This daughter, like her sisters and brothers, grew up to become one of my dearest friends. The day this daughter was born, I couldn't help but stare at her long, elegant fingers, her shock of lush eyelashes, and her thick mass of dark hair. *Oh my gosh*, I thought. I called one of my sisters from the hospital: "You'd better get down here. I think I just gave birth to your daughter. She looks so much like you!"

As she grew, she reminded me of this relative in terms of personality too. This was a huge compliment for both of them. Both are caring, strong, and sensitive, among other good things. I adore them! But their weak spots are also similar. Because of this, this sister and I have occasionally clashed, like instruments playing two different songs at the same time. We've had to work hard on our harmony. Consequently, we have eventually learned to make lots of beautiful music together. This took serious time.

Ironically, by the time this fourth child arrived, I thought, *I kind of know what I am doing. I am a fairly experienced mom. I have my mom's calm spirit fairly consistently dialed in, don't I? Childish temper tantrum? Been there. Seen that. When you're done, let's hug. Power struggle? I can side-step you most every time. Screaming? Meet your Zen master.*

But pride, as it is often wont to do, came before my fall.

I found myself falling into a few long-buried childhood struggle patterns with this daughter. Feelings would well up in me that had nothing to do with this sweet girl. I would sometimes let myself get sucked into the silliest little minor arguments. I didn't know exactly how to stop.

With prayer, I gradually realized the first step in letting go of my end of the tug-of-war rope was getting clear about who I was struggling with—it wasn't my daughter. She was strong-willed, but it was my relationship with a different strong-willed woman that still needed a little untangling.

Are you a parent who has struggled inexplicably with a child? Could it be that subconsciously you, too, may actually be struggling with someone else, someone who reminds you of your child? Someone you struggled with in childhood? Physical appearances and mannerisms are powerful. Check in with yourself and ask, "Is there a different relationship I need to figure out first, before I can figure out the one with this child?" I would encourage you to dig deep on this so you can avoid accidental self-fulfilling prophecy.

Here's another example. I have a friend whose daughter reminds her a lot of her mother. Some of the connotations of this are negative. But it's a bit of a "chicken and the egg" dilemma, isn't it? Was the daughter *truly* like the mother from the get-go, or was a negative connection (possibly based on appearance, mannerisms, and so on) accidentally created, labeled, and then reinforced over years? Who can say? But what we can say is that if we can untangle the primary relationship (from the family of origin) first, and *forgive*, then we can also more easily forgive similar foibles in the successive parent-child relationship.

But I digress. Let's circle back to the story about my daughter. One evening this sweet but strong-willed little girl offered me tender redemption. She was so young but so wise beyond her handful of years. The light bulb in my mind switched on that night, and the memory is still bright in my mind. "Time out!" I said with frustration over a transgression. "Go upstairs and do not come down!" I had crossed a mental line and had let myself get a little bit mean. She went to bed, sniffling. I knew I had hurt her feelings. I tried to tell myself I was justified. I wasn't.

A little later she called out for me. I went to her room and stood just outside the door. "Mommy," she said in her tiny voice, filled with so much love that it broke my heart a little. "Remember what Jesus said about children? Remember how people wanted them to be sent away, but He wouldn't do it? Remember how he wanted the children to come to him, to sit on his lap? Mommy, isn't that the right thing to do when children mess up? Don't they need someone to hold them, and teach them, even lots of times, to be good? Doesn't it take lots of times to learn to be all the way good?"

Yes. It takes lots of times to be all the way good, I thought, humbled. But a battle was going on in my soul. I was right, darn it! Wasn't I? But she was more right. Somehow, she understood a much higher law.

"A little child will lead them" (Isaiah 11:6). Was I willing to be led? Could I let go of my pride? Why was it so hard to let go? I stood outside of her door for a long time. Finally, I bowed my head and prayed. I listened to that still, small voice. "Let go," was the impression that came to me. "Be at peace."

I looked at my daughter with new, amazed eyes. She had been teaching me. I realized that she had come to Earth in part to bless me. In the years following, I still used time-outs but not as often. Instead, I tried to do what this daughter had taught me: to bring children close and teach, in non-contentious ways, in peaceful settings, about what is right. In other words, I tried to teach like Jesus.

Helping children learn goodness takes *a lot of gentle* repetition, of course. It pays off.

Today this daughter and I are the best of friends. She and her husband and two children are planning on moving close to us, joining three of her siblings (and their families) in the neighborhood or minutes away. (And more families are planning to join them!)

The recipe of one part firmness to two parts kindness and compassion is the best parenting recipe of which I am aware. As discussed in chapter 2, we are better able to extend firmness, kindness, and compassion to others when we are extending these very same things to ourselves on the regular.

Remember how hard it was to be a little child? You have feelings and needs, but you don't have articulation or decent self-regulation skills. You can only learn little by little, line upon line, precept upon precept. It takes time and so much practice. Children haven't been on earth long enough to figure out almost anything, including the "language" we most want them to learn. That language is called *Respect*.

Respect is a difficult language. It's nuanced—embracing politeness, patience, optimism and more. It takes overcoming parts of the "natural man" (see Mosiah 3:19). It can take years of practice to speak it fluently. Heavens, we know adults who are still grappling with this language. Many parents expect their young children to speak it immediately. But children are foreigners who have arrived on our planet without any words at all.

Imagine you are ten years old and have suddenly landed in France. You don't speak French. How would you prefer to be treated by French authority figures around you? Would you prefer to be scowled at, yelled at, or even asked to leave (think "time-out") for missteps vis a vis a language and culture with which you are not familiar?

Or would you prefer, whenever possible, to be extended grace? Would you like it if, when you violated a cultural code, someone took you aside (perhaps in quiet moments) and lovingly explained the correct phrasing or protocol? Of course, you would need repetition on these things so the teachings would stick.

What if your guides stuck it out with you? What if they were willing to gently teach the same principles over, and seemingly exponentially, over again? What if they would role play potential scenarios with you so you could be ready for the next challenges that might come along? And what if sometimes you really weren't "getting it" and you needed some "time out" to think things over? That could be a good thing too, right? You would still have your dignity intact. All of these things could be done under the umbrella of gentleness. (They forever can be).

There is a caveat here: children are naturally fascinated with power because they have so little. Don't "feed the beast." We gently teach toddlers, "You get what you get, and you don't get upset." We make sure and teach this in quiet, loving times too, so they can be ready to also hear us say it when they are actually upset. We can be firm and kind at the same time. Another thing I have been teaching my little granddaughters in quiet times is our motto, "More helping, less screaming."

Last Christmas we had a family brunch and Santa (one of our sons-in-law) came in full regalia. His little four-year-old didn't recognize him as her father. Santa asked, "Have you been good?" This little four-year-old, remembering our quiet goal-setting, announced, "Well, I have been trying to do less screaming and more helping." It was delightful—and true! She really had been trying hard.

We are all sent a little box of big powers from heaven. We all get to choose how we will use them. We have to be careful not to misuse them.

Once we had a little toddler who was occasionally teased by her younger sister, who had a more dominant personality than her older sister. Younger sister would tease to see if she could get "a rise" out of older sister. She was fascinated by her own personal power. The older sister, who came to earth with a very sensitive nature, would fall for the teasing continually.

One day I sat older, sensitive sister down with a little toy that squeaked when you squeezed it. I told her, "You won't be teased anymore if you 'stop squeaking'!" In other words, "If you don't respond when she teases, she will no longer have the 'payoff' from teasing you. With no payoff, she will learn that her powers do not work on you. She will eventually stop." This process took trial and much effort, but eventually, older sister did stop squeaking. The teasing got worse before it got better, in a last-ditch effort from teasing sister to get a "rise" out of the former squeaker. But as squeaky sister stayed strong at being calm, her teasing sister slowly lost interest in the teasing game.

All human behavior is seeking "payoff" of some kind. No payoff, no behavior (eventually). Pay off as many positive behaviors as you can. Try to ignore all the negative behaviors you can, or use time-out with as little emotion as possible. Children can also seek negative attention as they "play" with the "little box of powers" they receive as part of their mortal experience.

NOT YELLING 301

Okay, we've gone deeper. We have connected some of our behaviors to, possibly unconscious, emotional baggage we may be carrying. We've learned about being careful with our own parental powers in big ways. Now we can refine ourselves even more. This refinement happens at a more subtle, more spiritual level. It's Pilates—not for the physically deep core muscles, but for the deepest "core muscles" of our spirits.

Our oldest son helped me with this, asking one day if we could have a private conversation. I said, "Sure." We are big on requesting private conversations when we need to discuss something that is sensitive to another member of the family. This helps us keep dignity intact for all involved. We went into another room. Our son said that he had noticed that I was being very nice to one of the kids that he knew had been especially difficult for me in the last few weeks. "Yes," I said. I was being extra kind. Ironically, it was sort of "killing me softly" because, deep inside, I was actually resentful about a recurring negative behavior. I told him this.

"I think she can tell," he said. He told me that when he was a counselor at Anasazi[4] he was taught that if actions are right but the heart is wrong, kids will pick up on the subtle clues. Children are masters of observation. He was inspired to share this with me, I thought. I need to get my heart right with this child.

At first, I wasn't sure I could. I prayed hard for charity and forgiveness. The friendly feelings at last returned. But they were fragile. I wanted that love to be consistent. Focusing on avoiding contention, remembering the worth of children in the sight of God, and repenting on the regular helped me with that consistency.

Eventually, my feelings of pure love for this child became steadier and steadier. We became the best of friends once again.

NOT YELLING 400

For every thousand hacking at the leaves of evil,
there is one striking at the root.[5]
—Thoreau

We've covered a lot, haven't we? Now, let's go to the deepest level of all. Let's get to the root of evil and to the author of contention. Latter-day Saints, and those of many other faiths, believe that the author of contention is Satan, our adversary. It is he and his minions who tempt us to be contentious. Contention includes all kinds of awful things. Yelling is one manifestation.

Fortunately, good is ultimately more powerful than evil. Contention is a choice.

What exactly is contention? Because so much of what goes south in families comes from contention, let's get a good understanding of it. Many people only have a foggy understanding of contention. I get that. To be honest, even after a degree in biopsychology, I didn't clearly understand contention until I caught some "deep baseball" on the topic through the scriptures, counsel from Latter-day Saint apostles, and more.

Let's look at some super powerful, "cut-to-the-chase" clarifying scriptures on contention: "And ye will not suffer your children that they go hungry, or naked; neither will ye suffer that they transgress the laws of God, and fight and quarrel one with another, and serve the devil, who is the master of sin, or who is the evil spirit which hath been spoken of by our fathers, he being an enemy to all righ-teousness" (Mosiah 4:14).

In quiet moments we taught our children the scripture above and others like it. We especially taught them this one: "For verily, verily I say unto you, he that hath the spirit of contention is not of me, but *is of the devil, who is the father of contention, and he stir-reth up the hearts of men to contend with anger,* one with another" (3 Nephi 11:29; emphasis added).

Isn't this a fantastic scripture to memorize as a family? It tells the truth, and it's a truth children can handle. When we share truth with our children, truth bears witness of itself. Children can feel the truth of it. Then they can carry that witness and make choices, of their own accord, to follow it.

A man once asked the Prophet Joseph Smith how he was "enabled to govern so many people and to preserve such perfect order, remarking at the same time it was impossible for them to do it anywhere else.' Mr. Smith remarked that it was very easy to do that. 'How?' responded the gentleman; 'to us it is very difficult.' Mr. Smith replied, 'I teach them correct principles, and they govern themselves.'"[6]

Children, especially as they get older, really can govern them-selves (when it comes to contention and beyond), if they are served up the truth, with a generous side serving of love. Marjorie Hinckley (wife of former Latter-day Saint prophet Gordon B. Hinckley) said "yes" to children whenever possible. Of course, there are times of concern when this isn't possible, but everyone loves a "win." If we can say "yes" to creative ideas and moments of spontaneity, as well as, "Yes, you are right, thanks for teaching me," we can win the hearts of our children and teens as we show them deep respect.

There is a scripture that reads: "And he commanded them that there should be no contention . . . having their hearts knit together in unity and in love one towards another" (Mosiah 18:21).

Don't you just love that imagery of "hearts knit together in love"? This is the goal for families, and someday, for the world. How do we get there? The answer is that we can decrease contention by adding more charity, which is truly defined not just as a repository for funding for the poor, but as the pure love of Christ (see Moroni 7:47). Charity is the polar opposite of contention. How do we obtain such pure and undefiled love? This scripture gives us the answer: "Pray unto the Father with all the energy of heart, that ye may be filled with this love [charity], which he hath bestowed upon all who are true followers of his Son, Jesus Christ" (Mormon 7:48).There is more on charity at ChurchofJesusChrist.org.[7] Developing charity is hard work. I can testify that it's worth every second.

All happy families share a common desire to avoid contention. They sidestep temptations from the adversary to fight. Sure, there are tough topics that have to be discussed sometimes. But this can be done with respect, grace, and, whenever possible, with contention's kryptonite: the hug. I recall a tough day a handful of years ago with two of our then tweenagers. We had already raised six tweens by then, so you would think I wouldn't be fazed. But every tween offers a little unique testing of their own. On this day I was frustrated. One of our older daughters, Emily, noticed this. She saw my pursed, frustrated expression out of the corner of her eye. I wanted to tell her, "It's nothing, really."

And it wasn't a huge deal. I just wanted to drop a couple of at-the-moment super annoying tween-agers out of a window (a first-floor window, into the softest possible bushes).

My daughter approached me slowly, looking at me straight on. Raising her eyebrows, she said quietly, "Snuggles, not struggles, Mom. Remember?" There was a hint of teasing laughter in her sparkling eyes.

Yes, we are a huggy, snuggly sort of family. What is life without hugs? One of my best friends, Theresa, and I share this hugging thing. Years ago, a woman observed us hugging people right and left. "You two are hugger muggers," she said. We guessed she was on to something. But if 'hugging mugging' was wrong, we didn't want to be right.

This daughter was nudging me back into hug-e-ostasis (homeostasis with hugs). Then she said something that we could all write on mental Post-it notes when we have upset feelings: "Forgive them, Mom. We're all bumbling through life. We all make perceived mistakes. Don't let pride get in the way. Don't let the temptation to be contentious steal joy. You know it's the adversary tempting you. You can sidestep this as you most often do. Hug them." She was right, of course. It's difficult to hold on to frustrated feelings when you are giving someone a hug.

Science embraces hugging for many reasons: Hugs increase the bonding hormone oxytocin in the body. Hugs lower levels of anxiety and loneliness. Hugs can change blood pressure and heart rates. In an experiment at the University of North Carolina, Chapel Hill researchers found that "participants who didn't have any contact with their partners developed a quickened heart rate of 10 beats per minute compared to the five beats per minute among those who got to hug their partners during the experiment."[8] Wow.

We come to Earth as children of God to be tried and tested. When we arrive, so innocent and new, we are hoping for hugs. Lots of hugs. Endless years of hugs.

My husband and I had a basket full of children, and when they were small, they would often land on the same couch, falling all over each other like puppies. Those puppy childhood years may have sped past, but innocent laughter has never left. We have tried hard to maintain a home that is as innocent as possible.

In our case, this meant, in part, that the kids were raised mostly with little media. Consequently, they had to chat with each other frequently. Maybe this contributed to their solid friendships, built on years of silliness, serious debates, inside jokes, and hugs. Still, annoyance reared and rears its occasional head.

It's been said that when you are dealing with a difficult person, the first five minutes of your next encounter with them is the most important. This initial time sets the tone for the rest of the interaction. A big smile, a compliment, a little silliness, and of course some hugs can go a long way.

When the tweens came back, I hugged them. They were surprised. I was a little surprised. But I could tell by my older daughter's quiet confidence that she was not surprised. She trusted me to remember what works, and it did work. Peace was back, like a friend we had been missing.

In my early mothering years, I would sometimes go outside, throw up my hands to the heavens, and say, leaning in the direction of home, "Do you see that I am not yelling, or trying to spark any other kind of contention in that house? Do you see the hugging?"

Heaven saw me. I could feel it. I testify that those heavenly beings have seen you too. They see all of us, in all of those private, difficult moments of testing. They see us being firm but kind. They love us beyond measure. They are cheering on our efforts to be charitable.

Truly this kind of love, this charity, is the indispensable "construction adhesive" we need to build the strongest possible homes.

NUTS & BOLTS

- Assess your yelling tendencies. Could they decrease? Could constant prayer help? If you think that maybe it could, try it. This can work no matter your faith, or even with no faith at all.
- Remember that patience is a mental muscle. It gets stronger with practice.
- Gently teach your family about what contention is, where it comes from, and how to avoid it.
- Is there someone in your family who reminds you (in a negative way) of someone from your family of origin? If so, you can untangle the emotional knots with that person. This will help you then untangle knots with the person you love in your current family.
- Teach toddlers: "You get what you get, and you don't get upset." Memorize this together in quiet, peaceful moments.
- Avoid a "heart of war." Strive for a "heart of peace."
- Recipe for resolving a temper tantrum: one part firmness, one part compassion, one part kindness.
- All human behaviors are seeking payoff. Are we accidentally paying off incorrect behaviors with negative attention?

- Try to ignore negative behaviors when possible. Children are "playing" with their little "box of powers" from heaven and may choose negative attention if it's available.
- Reward all possible positive behaviors with praise and hugs and gratitude.

NOTES

1. Michael J. Fox, https://www.brainyquote.com/quotes/michael_j_fox_189302
2. Leo Tolstoy, *Anna Karenina*, by Leo Tolstoy—Project Gutenburg, May 22, 2020; https://www.gutenberg.org/files/1399/1399-h/1399-h.htm.
3. David O. McKay, *Stepping Stones to an Abundant Life*, comp. Llewelyn R. McKay [1971], 294.
4. Anasazi is a highly rated non-profit organization that hosts wilderness retreats for at-risk youth. You can learn more about their work at anasazi.org.
5. Henry David Thoreau, "Walden," by Henry David Thoreau—Project Gutenburg, January 1995; https://www.gutenberg.org/files/205/205-h/205-h.htm.
6. *Teachings of the Presidents of the Church: Joseph Smith*, https://www.churchofjesuschrist.org/study/manual/teachings-joseph-smith/chapter-24?lang=eng.
7. Gospel Topics, "Charity," https://www.churchofjesuschrist.org/study/manual/gospel-topics/charity?lang=eng.
8. Lindsay Holmes, "7 Reasons Why We Should Be Giving More Hugs," *The Huffington Post*, December 7, 2017; https://www.huffpost.com/entry/health-benefits-of-huggin_n_5008616.

Chapter Two
Building Happi-nest

*My housekeeping style can be best described as:
'There appears to have been a struggle'*
—Anon

* * *

Simplicity is the greatest sophistication[1]
—Leonardo Da Vinci

Basic order creates a more heavenly ambience in our increasingly strong homes. Have you noticed that when you experience "a bit of heaven" in a home, or somewhere else, you never forget it? I felt that heavenly feeling the first time I entered a Latter-day Saint home. The feeling was a melange of serenity and joy. I felt it again when I entered a Latter-day Saint temple. I've learned that you can feel it even in a home filled with busy children, even when things are a bit chaotic. This feeling stays with you.

For example, a friend of mine grew up in a strong Latter-day Saint home. She told me that when she broke up with a high school boyfriend he said, "Well, I am going to miss you, but I am really going to miss the feeling in your house. That was the best feeling." My friend had nine younger siblings! It definitely wasn't perfect. But her boyfriend had felt a peace in that home. He couldn't name it, but he had felt it.

This is the feeling we want in our homes as often as possible. This feeling is achievable as we recognize and avoid contention (see previous chapter) and find other ways to try to recreate a little of the heaven we left behind (see the last chapter on "Building Heaven"). This book is full of tools to do this. One of these tools is basic order. I love the following scripture: "My house is a house of order, saith the Lord, and not a house of confusion" (D&C 132:8). My house is still confused in places, but we believe!

Most adults believe in order. Babies and toddlers are not fully converted. They are order atheists. Along these lines, I have an idea for you. If you are the first to materialize and sell the following, it's all yours! Here is the idea: Create a piece of art that depicts a lot of adorable, happy babies in hardhats, like unto construction workers. The hard hats are just slightly too big, and they are askew—a dip here, an eye covered there. Some babies are holding tiny tools like hammers and wrenches. Other tools are scattered on the ground around them. At the bottom of this piece there is a statement that reads, "Please pardon our mess. Eternal beings under construction." I wish I could offer one of these plaques to every young family. It's impossible to always maintain ideal order as tiny children are growing. We need to allow ourselves lots of grace.

That said, the power of a basically ordered, basically tasteful, basically calm home cannot be underestimated in the life of a child. Children remember the efforts we make in these areas their entire lives. If we are even trying at all, their future adult selves will be so thankful. Conversely, if children don't have their basic home life needs met, this absence can influence their worldview.

For example, in 1992 Gloria Steinem gave an impressively open and honest interview with *Vanity Fair*. She discussed her home life as the only child of a divorced and mentally ill single mother. Ms. Steinem said that she grew up in "a dilapidated, rat-infested, virtually empty farmhouse a few feet from a major highway. . . . I don't know why it took me so long to realize you need to have a home."[2]

Today Ms. Steinem lives in an upper east side Brownstone in New York City. She has purchased connecting apartments and decorated them thoughtfully. Her bedroom includes a canopied bed. "It's so satisfying to feel as though I have a home!" she said.

I am so happy for her, and I also think I understand why she didn't hesitate, at one time, to encourage women to leave their homes. She had never known how sweet it could be to work from home sometimes, or just be home. She had never known a real home. I am so very grateful for all Ms. Steinem did to advance the cause of women. She was there when we needed her. Now her home is there for her, and she realizes she needs it. We all need that feeling of home.

If we move from Ms. Steinem's negative recollection of her childhood home all the way to the other end of the spectrum, we might find something more like a particular scene I am thinking of from the film *A Hundred-Foot Journey*. In this scene, a family from India is in need of some assistance. Their car has broken down, and a lovely, generous French girl takes them to her home and feeds them. Her level of graciousness is so impressive it's nearly surreal. But it's also kind of inspiring.

She serves them homegrown food that is clearly sumptuous and delectable. You can nearly smell the pungent salty cheeses and olives. You can almost taste the crunch of fresh crudites. The food has been gathered in from family harvests. Her manner is warm and effusive.

The home is clean and well-appointed. You can imagine the touch of a spring breeze blowing gently through linen curtains on French windows. Clutter is not an invited guest. Beautiful simplicity is everywhere. You just want to go there and be wrapped up in all the heaven of that home. You don't want to leave!

Even though we have come far, I still have more road ahead as I ever strive to gently create more order and ambience at home. I am working at it—not in a frenzied, perfectionistic way, but just a little bit at a time.

If you are a parent of young children right now, I have strong feelings of love and empathy for you. The key word in this season is *grace*. Keep going. You are amazing. You are doing the hardest job, and you are doing it largely without accolades. There is so much involved in the construction of eternal beings.

When I was where some of you are now, I would sometimes call my husband when he was at work and tell him that he could "have it all," just not all at once. Sometimes I would leave silly messages in his voice mail, offering him choices of what he could have that night:

1. A clean house
2. A delicious meal
3. A glamorous version of me, or
4. Children who were recently showered with extra high levels of attention.

Sometimes he got more than one of these items on the same day, but I never wanted him to expect them all on the same day. As Shakespeare said, "Expectations are the root of all suffering."[3] I wanted to under-promise but over-deliver when I could.

Back then we had a lot of young children, and I had a small organizational skill set. We had a few routines but needed more. Eventually, we got them. We also needed more order. We got this too but not right away. There was a time when searching for missing items felt like a mommy-toddler part-time job.

Once, and I am not kidding, I was headed out the door to church (my husband had left earlier to attend meetings), and I was so desperate to find the car keys that I wondered if I could use something else as a key. I actually removed a large barrette from my daughter's hair, opened it up, placed it in the ignition, and turned on the car. It worked. It really, truthfully, worked! I feel like this little miracle was a tender, limited-edition mercy from a gracious God. He had not forgotten his slightly frenzied, but trying, daughter.

I am now a rabid believer in the power and beauty of order. I am a zealot about the ability of basic order, in our homes and our appearances, to bring a sense of calm. I have seen my husband and children visibly calm down and relax *just because I brushed my hair and put on mascara*. It's subconscious for them. I don't think they have ever noticed the connection. But I have, over and over. Why does a little good grooming help everyone be more cooperative? I think it is because order and loveliness connect us to heaven. We are wired to love truly heavenly things.

When people and things around us are tidy, we all seem to inwardly sigh peacefully. Just the sound of a vacuum cleaner buzzing or a humming dishwasher can make everything feel better. When I was growing up, sometimes there was sibling fighting and other negative stress. But it seemed that when the dishwasher was turned on and the family was tucked in for the night, everything would somehow be okay. I felt the same way on Saturday mornings. I would open my window to hear the sound of the lawn mower munching away. I would deeply inhale the delightful ever-spring scent of freshly mowed grass. How could the world not be wonderful when fathers were mowing lawns and creating such delightful fragrances for the noses of little girls to savor?

We can also follow nature's example of engaging all our senses on the insides of our homes. Even with small budgets, we can add music for our ears, art for our eyes, soft things to touch, lovely aromas, and healthy, delicious tastes. When many/all of our senses are happily engaged and there is peace in our hearts at home, it really can feel like heaven.

I wish I was a natural organizer like Marie Kondo or a post-jail Martha Stewart. In fact, in the world of Marthas, there is a Martha from the New Testament I really admire. I know, everyone likes Mary best in this true story. I get it. She seems like a person who loves to listen and might not be wild about chores. But here's the thing: I am also not wild about chores, and I love listening.

Given the choice between making someone dinner and chatting with someone about dinner or anything spiritual, I would rather chat. This would be especially true, of course, if the person I was chatting with were our Lord and Savior Jesus Christ.

This doesn't mean I don't like to make dinner or host dinner parties. I do. I love to cook. I love to jazz up a table and surroundings for parties. I love hospitality. I am just saying that I am more "Mary dominant" than "Martha dominant." I see many "Martha dominant" women in the world zipping around (with time I don't seem to have) with Pinteresting flair, and I think, "I want more of that." Do you need someone to chat with about your feelings? I may suddenly have all the time in the world.

Over the years, I have become better at Martha things. The Fly Lady website has been an incredible help. If you are totally overwhelmed with household things, this is a great place to start.

It has taken time to grow from grace to grace, to saying grace at a gracefully set table. I have relied on the promise of this scripture: "And if men come unto me I will show unto them their weakness. I give unto men weakness that they may be humble, and my grace is sufficient for all men that humble themselves before me; for if they humble themselves before me, and have faith in me, then will I make weak things become strong unto them" (Ether 12:27). I am grateful the Savior can not only make up for what we lack if we come unto Him, but He can also make our weaknesses the strongest things about us.

With mighty prayer and time, I have become better at things such as decluttering and, even better, at not cluttering in the first place. I've learned to put away things (like keys) in the same place each time. Our family has gone from sometime CHAOS (Can't Have Anyone Over Syndrome) to HEY! (Hello! Enter, Y'all!).

I worked hard to figure out how to get kids ready for events with less mess, more peace, and less drama. Nervous kids can be painfully good at drama. I created a family declaration: "Departures without drama!" I would say this with enough volume to be heard over the herd as we headed out.

One solution required thinking not just outside the box but also inside a closet. Specifically, I dubbed a closet "the Sunday closet" (this could be called by another name, like "the occasion closet"). I reserved Thursdays for updating the Sunday closet. I would slice off a chunk of this day to wash, iron, and restock.

In this closet I kept all of my little one's Sunday outfits, including socks, shoes, hair items, and back-up extras of these items. In this closet, I also kept our Sunday bag, which was filled with the usual suspects: diapers, wipes, snacks, and Sunday "quiet toys" for sacrament meeting. Initially, I was nursing a tendency to overpack. This produced a very large Sunday bag. One Sunday a friend asked me if I was raising another child in this bag.

I loved that bag, those children, and that Sunday closet. Time and time again it saved me. Where there had once been departures for church filled with sounds of children calling into the air, "Where are my shoes?" now there were actual, immediate shoes. There they were! Staring back at me from the closet! Next to all the other easy-access Sunday things.

Immediately upon returning from church or another special event, I required all our little people to change into other clothing and to hand over all the Sunday things. Then I would return them to the Sunday closet. Sigh of relief. It was peace on earth, closet edition!

Great domestic peace enters our homes as clutter departs. I knew I was growing a bit more in this area when a friend called one day to tell me she had some amazing toys her older children no longer needed. She wanted to share them with me. At first, I was thrilled. Free toys! We had so many tiny children then, and our budget was also small. This seemed like a windfall. Our many children would be so excited! I drove up to her house, and we loaded the boxes of toys into my car. The toys turned out to be a mad plethora of tiny things, such as Barbie shoes. Inwardly, I cringed. My friend was so generous. I thanked her sincerely, but I couldn't drive home. This wasn't a windfall. This was a clutter windstorm.

Worried, I kept driving around, not heading home. I was already saving my baby daily from choking on things. These Barbie shoes were baby hand grenades. I sank a little deeper into thought. Abraham Lincoln didn't even have Lincoln logs. He had few books. Basically, he must have played outside all day. I decided he had turned out okay. I thought of my Uncle Bill. One of his favorite phrases was, "When in doubt, throw it out!" Uncle Bill had helped in the development of the fetal heart monitor. He had been a rower in the Olympics twice. He had to know something. I was in doubt. It was time to throw things out, or at least out of my life. I drove to Goodwill and gave them every box my friend had just given me.

Saying goodbye to things can turn out to be endorphin central. No tchotchke purchase can compete with the feeling of losing pounds of clutter weight. The first time I drove up to the blue Goodwill truck, I truly had to restrain myself from hugging the people who took my stuff. They were saving me. They didn't judge my worn items; they didn't mind if the bags were hard to lug. They just smiled and asked me if I wanted a tax receipt. "No thanks, the government needs the money!" I said as I waved and drove away. I often feel that I should pay the people at Goodwill.

When we're in our younger years, many of us play a game I call "Acquire." We're so poor that acquiring/owning lots of "things" just sounds great. Then we get too many things, and the things start to own us. The game switches to "Begone." We try to get as much stuff out of our homes as possible. This is especially true with growing families as children move through different developmental stages.

Our "home system" shares similarities with human "digestive systems." When things are running smoothly, things come into the home and things go out again (to the garbage or donation centers) on a regular, ongoing basis. There is "flow," a comfortable rhythm: things in, things out on the regular. The house is healthy and vibrant.

When many things come in but too few things go out, there is imbalance and stagnation. We know this feeling. We can't stuff one more thing into that cupboard or closet. Life itself may start to feel heavy and oppressive. I've noticed that if I don't give or throw things away on a regular basis, the house starts to feel "backed up." With fewer things, life is simply simpler. But getting there can be hard.

Steve Jobs once said, "Simplicity can be harder than complex. You have to work hard to get your thinking clean to make it simple. But it's worth it in the end because once you get there, you can move mountains."[4]

Simplicity is highly correlated with love, joy, delight, connection, unity, and being able to find your car keys instantly.

The best book many of us have found on this topic is *The Life-Changing Magic of Tidying Up: The Japanese Art of Decluttering and Organizing* by Marie Kondo. She also has a show. Her bottom line is, throw (almost) everything away. All the things. The user manuals, the chipped figurines, the gifts you never liked. Basically everything, unless, she says, it "sparks joy" in you.

This "sparks joy" rule changed my life. It led me back to those welcoming blue bins at Goodwill again and again. The remaining items remind me that joy is all around me.

Fine tuning this process took more leaps of faith. For example, at one time I had a collection of expensive "current" organizational products. I wasn't actually using them, but maybe I would someday. Could I toss these trending treasures? Since I had no clearly defined place to store them, I would periodically move them to new places, reminding me of the iconic "rearranging of deck chairs on the *Titanic*." It was silly! Our ship called *Home* was still too heavy. I needed to "stuff the stuff overboard." I did—and I do, again and again.

Organization is "well planned hoarding," according to the minimalists. I don't want to live with one plate and one glass and one fork, but I agree with them that less is more. But still, extreme less is less exciting, right? This is why I love *The Minimal Mom* on YouTube. She's not too extreme, and she has great ideas. (I am not nearly as minimal as she is, but she does inspire me.)

When things are simplified, we're not tearing through piles to find that one thing without which we are going to be late to that other thing. We're not as tempted to be frantic.

That feeling of cleanliness, order, and light, whenever we can get it, is such a happy feeling. It's a heavenly feeling. We are in love with heavenly things because, in the deepest part of ourselves, we know we came from heaven.

So we desire a measured number of lovely, ordered things in our homes. We want to create a home that signals simplicity and comfort. We grow from "grace to grace," and a graceful home is what we are growing toward over time. It will be a home that will be remembered with fondness.

If you have tiny children right now, let's be real. You often feel exhausted. You know how exhaustion feels like no one else. You deserve all the grace, all the heavenly applause. You are doing the most important job on Earth, and often you are doing it on little sleep. You may feel the weight of what "still needs to be done." But to your family, what you are already doing may feel like more than enough.

For example, ten years ago, our family added a precious seven-year-old Native American girl to our then family of seven children. This shift in our family dynamics threw us completely. We knew of this new daughter's former circumstances and were prepared to be in over our heads, but we were in way over our heads. When we weren't logistically dog-paddling through her appointments and court dates, we spent a lot of time taking comfort in routine. She was watching.

One Saturday morning the kitchen was its usual noisy hub. We were making, eating, and spilling all the pancake things. The scent of sizzling bacon wafted through the air. Frank Sinatra's voice, smooth as butter, was in the background. There was a lot of "Please pass the syrup!" and "Seriously?" as stories and quips were exchanged. There were occasional annoyances. There was random singing. There was laughter and chatter.

It was a convention of morning larks chirping away. Attire favored fleece pajamas. Not a single hair was brushed. No make-up, no shaving. We were a silly, scruffy bunch.

About four bites of pancakes in, our newest and youngest daughter beckoned me to move into the living room. She wanted to speak to me alone. I didn't want to go, but her imploring look persuaded me. I followed her into the living room and then leaned down a little to adjust to her height. I didn't have to lean far. She was tall for her age. "What do you need?" I asked.

"I just want to tell you something," she said. "It feels . . ."

She looked down. Was she wondering if she should say it?

"This house . . . here . . . it just . . . well . . . it feels like. . . heaven." Her eyes were round and deep. She was serious. I glanced from her to the kitchen where pancake batter had dribbled from the pouring style mixing bowl onto the stove. The sink was filled with breakfast dishes. I took stock of our messy kids, our sometimes messy lives. Heaven had to be more together than this.

I looked back at her with a skeptical raised eyebrow. But now there were tears in those big round eyes. Realization spread over me. She saw us in a different way. She had not always been able to count on safety. She had not always known the warmth of consistent light in her life. We thought of ourselves as ordinary. But to her, a secure home was extraordinary.

Through her eyes, I saw our family differently. We weren't Pinterest material, but did it matter? I hugged her with all the protective love I could muster. She slipped her hand in mine, and we went back to the kitchen. Morning light was pouring in through the windows, illuminating a plethora of breakfast crumbs on the wood floors and warming us to the core.

I love what Jaeden taught us about gathering. While there is no place for perfectionism in our basically ordered (but sometimes not) homes, working *toward* simplicity and order helps with our natural desire to gather often.

The importance of gathering cannot be underestimated. Life was never meant to be a time of endless wool-gathering (as one might say in the sixteenth century). But apparently, it was meant to be a time of much gathering. What comes to mind when you hear the word *gather*? Gathering with family and friends? Meeting with your faith group or attending a community event? Or maybe something broader, like the gathering of Israel? Or something historic, like Jesus gathering with His followers?

Maybe, as it often is for me, it's remembering that poignant, poetic line from our Savior: "O Jerusalem, Jerusalem, which killest the prophets, and stones them that are sent unto thee; how often would I have gathered thy children together, as a hen *doth gather* her brood under *her* wings, and ye would not!" (Matthew 23:37; emphasis added). He would have gathered them (and all of us), if given the smallest (free-agency driven) chance. The Savior is all about feelings of peace, protection, and *joie de vivre* that can come from gathering.

Latter-day Saint President Russell M. Nelson has asked us to gather. He has asked the Saints to gather at home and in the temple, or the Lord's house, a place where we can feel close to our ancestors sometimes. We are counseled to create homemade circles of love like family home evening and devotionals (see later chapters). In these places that "feeling" can be strong. Being knee-deep in genuine, peaceful love and acceptance, surrounded by those who know and love you best, is sublime. It's worth all the efforts.

Gathering often creates a wonderful circle of something: think of a soft ruffle on the hem of a toddler's skirt, a circle of elephants united in empathy, or "circling the wagons." The Lord describes His work as "one eternal round" and being "encircled about eternally in the arms of His love."

When gathering material, we lay down loose stitching on a flat piece of fabric. Then we gently pull one end of the threads until all the fabric ruffles together. It's exciting to see the transformation. Once gathered, the material becomes more "alive," more interesting, more fun.

What is the thread that Latter-day Saints believe can gather us all together in the gospel? It's the Spirit, or the gift of the Holy Ghost. Emotionally and spiritually this thread pulls us all in a little closer. The Saints ever seek to gain and keep this gift.

Why is this gift so powerful? The Latter-day Saint prophet Joseph Smith said this about it:

> It quickens all the intellectual faculties, increases, enlarges, expands and purifies all the natural passions and affections; and adapts them, by the gift of wisdom, to their lawful use. It inspires, develops, cultivates and matures all the fine-toned sympathies, joys, tastes, kindred feelings, and affections of our nature. It inspires virtue, kindness, goodness, tenderness, gentleness, and charity. It develops beauty of person, form and features. It tends to health, vigor, animation, and social feeling. It invigorates all the faculties of the physical and intellectual man. It strengthens, and gives tone to the nerves. In short, it is, as it were, marrow to the bone, joy to the heart, light to the eyes, music to the ears, and life to the whole being.[5]

We are wired to gather, to feel these things. As one of my favorite authors Brené Brown has said, "As humans we are hard-wired to connect with others, it's what gives purpose and meaning to our lives and without it there is suffering."[6] We bring the people. The Holy Ghost brings the warmth, peace, and joy.

What if people don't know about the Holy Ghost or are not interested in utilizing its power? In our drive to unite, people sometimes seek other, more precarious ways to connect. For example, isn't it interesting that *spirits* is an old-fashioned word that was once used to describe alcohol? Some bars have even been called "speakeasies." The use of "spirits" is an attempt to re-create feelings of ease that come from the true spirit of God, or the gift of the Holy Ghost. The true spirit of God makes it easier to speak, minus the danger and addiction that can accompany "spirits." It's the most honest of threads that can honestly connect us. It's the true gatherer: no side effects, no hangovers, no regrets. It's peace, without the bottle and the price tag. It's freedom.

Latter-day Saints believe it is a joy to seek to gather with the true "gatherer," the Holy Ghost, as we prepare for the most glorious gathering of all ahead: reuniting with God and our family in heaven, in that circle of love that will never end. The ambience there will feel like love, all the time.

NUTS & BOLTS

- If you have small children, you have "eternal beings under construction." Give yourself lots of grace!
- Latter-day Saints believe that heaven was lovely and clean ("heavenly"). Whenever we are creating heavenly surroundings on earth, we are trying to re-create our experience there.
- Personal grooming can help everyone be more cooperative. If we look a little more heavenly, we may get a more heavenly response.
- Addressing all the ambient senses brings a little more heaven to our homes.

- Consider creating a "Sunday closet."
- Goodwill is our friend.
- Gathering imperfectly and bonding with our family members beats obsessive cleaning and perfectionism every time.
- Check out the Fly Lady website for great routines to make home keeping easier.

NOTES

1. Clare Boothe Luce, *Stuffed Shirts* (New York, NY: Ayer Co Pub, 1971), 239.
2. Leslie Bennetts, "The Philosophy of Gloria Steinem, Patron Saint of American Feminism," *Vanity Fair*, September 4, 2013; https://www.vanityfair.com/culture/1992/01/gloria-steinem-feminism-book.
3. "Basics of Buddhism," PBS. Public Broadcasting Service, 2021. https://www.pbs.org/edens/thailand/buddhism.htm.
4. Steve Jobs, "In Quotes: Apple's Steve Jobs." BBC News. BBC, October 6, 2011; https://www.bbc.com/news/world-us-canada-15195448.
5. Joseph Smith, *Key to the Science of Theology*, 9th ed. [1965], 101.
6. Brené Brown, *Daring Greatly: How the Courage to Be Vulnerable Transforms the Way We Live, Love, Parent and Lead* (London, England: Portfolio Penguin, 2013), 4.

Chapter 3

Building Service Opportunities

I can not do all the good that the world needs.
But the world needs all the good that I can do.[1]
—Jana Stanfield

* * *

Service is the only door out of the prison of oneself.
—Anonymous

Acts of service are the metaphorical bricks in our homes. It's hard for the adversary to "blow down" houses built on Christ-like, loving service.

You know about the Latter-day Saints/family connection. You may also know about the Latter-day Saint/service connection. A quick Google search will reveal "Latter-day Saint Helping Hands," "Latter-day Saint Charities" and more. The Saints show up around the world to help when disasters strike. They come organized and prepared. When a flood victim asked how she could possibly thank her Latter-day Saint rescuers they replied, "Oh don't worry about it. We love to serve." It's true—for most Latter-day Saint adults. Children are another story. Developing a love for service doesn't usually come easily for children, even though service is at the heart of every well-oiled machine of a home. Children are great examples of the scripture that says "the spirit is willing, but the flesh is weak" (Matthew 26:41).

For example, one day our then four-year-old son cozied up to me and said, "Oh, Mommy, I love you so much! I love you so much that I would do anything for you!"

Wow, I thought as I stood there folding laundry. *He said "anything"!*

"Would you please fold this laundry?" I asked. He considered.

"What day is today?" he said.

"It's Tuesday," I replied.

He squared his tiny shoulders and smiled. "Mommy, I would do anything for you. Except on Tuesdays!"

All of us start out with the "natural man."[2] It takes a while to move from the self-centeredness of babyhood to "other centeredness."

The Saints not only believe that loving, interdependent service within families is paramount, but they also believe that teaching children to have "service focused hearts" will help them to navigate their futures with compassion and charity. Service strikes a preemptive blow against the teenage narcissism creep and helps steer focus away from self and toward God. As it says in the Book of Mormon, "When ye are in the service of your fellow beings, ye are only in the service of your God" (Mosiah 2:17).

Behavior is always trying to move in the direction of our strongest thoughts and beliefs. So we teach little Saints songs with lyrics like, "When we're helping we're happy, and we sing as we go; and we love to help mother, for we all love her so."[3]

God provides service opportunities for grown-ups too. The Church of Jesus Christ of Latter-day Saints is a lay church, and nearly everyone has a calling, which is a responsibility for something related to the ward. For example, my husband, Tom, was just released as our ward bishop. While he was bishop, he also had a demanding full-time job, one child headed for college, and one child still in high school. Maybe being this busy is God's "stay out of trouble" plan. He keeps us all too busy for a lot of sinning!

Fortunately, Tom was not snowed under. He had a volunteer team of people serving the ward. All callings of this kind are temporary and rotational. In a handful of years, someone else will be the bishop. Someone else will be in charge of the nursery. Other women will be called to the ward Young Women presidency. Other men will run the ward Young Men organization, and so on. This inspired system engenders humility and helps people learn a wide variety of service skills.

CHORES

Children don't do what you expect.
They do what you inspect.
—Marie Ricks

The opportunity for service that hits closest to home is, of course, chores. The word that I associate most closely with chore success is *delegation*. Delegation is freedom. Delegation takes work. It's said that "a lazy mother picks up after her children." I picked up after a lot of children until I internalized the importance of this quote. Let's be honest—I still pick up after people but not nearly as much as I once did. I have learned that smart delegation is a key to a better life. I am a massive fan of delegation. If I could somehow delegate the typing of the next paragraph of this book to you, I might do it.

Smart delegation is not demanding things with a side of yelling. Smart delegation is a subtle art, requiring practiced finesse. It takes time to learn to do it well. I am still learning. It also requires the release of some pride. Sometimes we want to just do it all ourselves, but we lose things when we take this approach:

- We get less done in the end. The efficiency of trained family members can take huge time burdens from us.
- We lose the chance for our children to feel the self-confidence that service naturally provides.
- We lose the chance to help family members feel more needed and valued at home.
- We lose the chance to help family members love us and other family members more. The ancient truth is oft worth repeating: "We love those whom we serve."

If we are "all in" for delegation, where do we start? This was the question I found myself scratching my head about when I was desperate for help in the chore department as a young mom. I felt in over my head, surrounded by tiny, unprofessional, albeit adorable, tousled heads.

I was blessed and cursed to have grown up with housekeepers. For a good handful of those years, the rotating housekeepers lived in a guest suite in the downstairs of our home. Maria, and each of the housekeepers who had preceded her in the job, cooked and cleaned and were very nice to us in general. I sometimes felt guilty about this. I would often get up and make my bed before a maid could get there. This was basically my entire experience with chores. Sad, huh?

When I became a mom, I no longer had a "Maria." Or did I? I looked at my children and saw "potential Maria's." I could—you guessed it—delegate! It took a lot of time and some training, but they got the chore thing down. One thing I had to be careful about was not expecting too much. They were, after all, children. I learned this lesson one day when I asked our younger son to work on some pantry straightening. When he called to me later to see his work, I frowned. There was a lot left undone. He immediately saw the frown, and his head dropped. He was so sad to have disappointed me. Then I was so sad to have disappointed him with my response. He had tried so hard! I made a vow then and there to always praise the good whenever chores were done. I vowed to expect the basics but not be too particular.

A key to chore training success can be summed up in three words: praise, praise, praise. When chores are first being established, external rewards are great. Praise may be even better. I have a friend who is in her fifties and still loves cleaning bathrooms because she was praised so much for being good at it as a child. Our teen daughter still sets up and decorates for celebration meals. We praise her for being good at this because she is. Look for their skills, figure out which tasks align with those skills, and then praise them to the moon and back for helping. It works!

In early years, I also tried to dig deep into my children's potential guilt soil with a little poetry "seed planting." I think the following is the first poem we all memorized together during a devotional. This was, I guess, my first "chores public relations platform"—a TED talk-ish poem before TED talks!

Which Loved Best?
by Joy Allison (1917)

"I love you, Mother," said little John;
Then, forgetting his work, his cap went on.
And he was off to the garden swing,
Leaving his mother the wood to bring.

"I love you, Mother," said rosy Nell,
"I love you better than tongue can tell."
Then she teased and pouted full half the day.
Till her mother was glad when she went to play.

"I love you, Mother," said little Fan,
"To-day I'll help you all that I can;
How glad I am that school doesn't keep!"
So she rocked the babe till he fell asleep.

Then stepping softly, she took the broom,
And swept the floor, and dusted the room.
Busy and happy all day was she;
Helpful and happy as a child could be.

"I love you, Mother," again they said,
Three little children going to bed.
How do you think that mother guessed
Which of them really loved her best?[4]

I admit, the poem above may not have actually ignited a passion for chores in our kids, but it has been the fodder for a lot of laughing and teasing about chores and about who the "favorite child" really was (answer: all of them).

Like all kids, mine were looking for ways to be done with chores as quickly as possible. This sometimes meant giving in to the temptation to stuff everything in a closet, hoping I wouldn't open the closet. I opened many a closet. I once heard a brilliant quote: "Children don't do what you expect. They do what you inspect."

My next "public relations" move, after the above poem memorizing, was to try to instill a particular truth in them. I am going to share this truth with you. It's an important one, and as we have discussed in previous chapters, internalizing truth is critical because our behaviors tend to move in the direction of our core beliefs.

Before I share it, I just want to share with you the amount of enthusiasm I gave this truth while distributing it among our small children: a ton. I expressed "Cosmo at a BYU game" level of enthusiasm. I really wanted them to get it.

So what is this awesome truth that I shared with them? It was simply this: "You will feel better and happier after you get your chores done because you can't truly enjoy your playtime until you have done some hard work first. If your life is all 'play,' the true happiness fades away! It's the 'exhale' of being done with the hard and relaxing into the fun that fills you with joy. If you don't know the hard, you can't recognize the easy, right? It's that feeling of being done that fills you with thrills! Then you are off to the races or the crafting or the kid movie or video game or what have you!" Then I did a back handspring, a la BYU's sports team mascot Cosmo, to emphasize my point. Just kidding!

I knew we had made headway with the kids internalizing this truth when our little son Jared said to me one day, "Could I please have some chores, Mommy?" When my surprised eyebrows said, "Why?" he insisted, "I need them because I want to have that feeling, Mommy! You know, when you feel so good after doing some really hard things like chores? But you can't have that feeling unless you do the hard things first!" Today this son is a hard-working investment banker.

Of course, rewards are awesome. They are far better than using negatives, as in, "If you don't do ____, you will lose ____." Sometimes negatives may feel like the only option. I understand. I remember being so frustrated with two young girls one day that I said, "If you don't stop this squabbling right now I am not going to pay for your wedding receptions!" You can imagine the non-impact that statement had on a two- and four-year-old. They didn't know what I was even really talking about. I didn't either! I was just so frustrated!

Thoughtful rewards work for all sorts of positive behaviors you want to instill. For example, I would tell our son that if he was obedient all week, then on Fridays we would swing by the little store in our area that sold Pokémon cards and he could buy a pack. We bought a lot of cards on Fridays.

What is interesting about all this is that years later he told me that he still rewarded himself with Pokémon cards. Even when he became an investment banker, he would sometimes purchase a pack of Pokémon cards on a Friday evening. I love it. He is married to a wonderful woman now. Maybe they will buy their children Pokémon cards one day.

Many parents use a reward strategy for good behaviors. It "works a treat," as they say in Britain. Be careful when rewarding with actual treats. Food as a reward can be problematic if done often. I think once in a while is all right, but not consistently because we don't want to accidentally create a Pavlovian link between behavior, treats, and possibly, later, emotional eating. There are so many other creative ways to reward children.

For example, D'Lonna Allred Nelson (BS, BYU '99) said, "It is amazing what kidney beans and a mason jar can do. It can inspire my four boys to clean a messy room, be kinder to each other, and get their homework done without complaining—all for a bean to put in a jar that, when filled, will be traded in for a family movie night, dinner of choice, or family bike ride."[5]

In any chore assigning situation, there is a technique that really helps. It comes from the world of sales, where we are trying to "assume the purchase." This is what you do: simply nod your head vertically up and down as you give the instructions. Your little ones will subconsciously nod too. This physical mimicking of your "we have an agreement" behavior helps them to agree too. It can help kids get ready for bed, do a little chore, and so on.

Another technique is to ask rather than tell. Instead of saying, "This is what needs to be done: jammies, teeth, and clothes laid out for tomorrow," we could ask instead, "What needs to be done next to get ready for tomorrow? What is the next thing we do at night?" Kids love to be the ones to explain to us what needs to happen next. It gives them a feeling of empowerment, and children don't have many chances to feel powerful.

I mentioned this in another chapter, but it bears repetition and even expansion. I made a connection over the years: when I was dressed and groomed pretty well, I got more chore cooperation with less push back. It's fascinating. Everyone even seems to be in a better mood when I take a little time to invest in my appearance. Of course, I get dressed every day. But sporting exercise wear with no makeup and no hair care is (who knew?) not all that inspiring. I really think my family is not even responding on a conscious level when I upgrade my presentation. It's more subconscious, and I think it goes back even as far as the premortality discussed earlier.

We sense that heavenly people are well groomed. Thus, another way we can bring more heaven into our homes is to try to represent it. But even at the temporal, daily grind level, we all just respond better to serving "bosses" who look like they care about themselves.

Children's confidence increases as they learn to serve one another in small ways at home. As the girls got older in our family, I would encourage them to plan and execute friend birthday parties for their younger siblings. They got to choose the games and the food and decor. I provided the funding. Sometimes they helped with the games at the parties. This meant lots of fun, but more important, lots of bonding.

As we grow in serving each other inside our homes, we can reach out to those outside of our homes. I remember my father piling us children into a car just before Christmas one year and taking us to a drug store where he insisted that we choose small gifts for the elderly. Then we drove to a nursing home deep in the heart of a less optimal part of Washington DC.

It was night time, and the nursing home felt new and scary. My siblings and I wanted to run. Dad told us to sing. Begrudgingly, we squeaked out a few songs.

The whole experience was awful, but ironically, I look back on it with fondness. I am in awe that my father took the time in his busy schedule to orchestrate that experience for us. He hung in there even when we complained. I now count it as one of my finest Christmas experiences. I have a special spot in my heart for the elderly—and, of course, for my dad.

We have a dear widowed neighbor. For years I have given our two youngest children flowers to take to her, for all kinds of occasions, or just because. They weren't always interested. I've had to insist a few times. But we have all felt the warmth of visiting with this good woman. We've taught our children that service, sooner or later, makes us smile.

Our children have taught us too. They often have abilities we don't have. They can fill in blanks in our lives. For example, one daughter helps us with family history, our finance major son teaches us about investments, our doctor son helps us with our health, and our event planner daughter has helped me with family events.

I haven't always recognized their helping strengths. One of our daughters who came with excellent administration skills drove me nuts when she was a child because she often wanted to be in charge of many of our schedules. I didn't want to be bossed around by a nine-year-old. "I am the boss of me," I wanted to shout in a toddler voice. Instead, I would often square my shoulders and remind her that "I am the mom." But somewhere along the way I realized she really could help me. I finally let her. When she wanted to take phone calls for me and write down messages, I let her. Today she organizes family reunion details and is there in a New York minute when I need a project assistant.

If you have a child who is making you crazy, stop for a minute and ask, "What could be the hidden future gift in this behavior?"

Is my restless child a future entrepreneur? Is my bull-headed child a future leader? There may be gifts yet to be revealed.

What is also interesting is that the kids have blessed each other with their gifts. Emily, our English major, has helped many a sibling with a job resume. Our doctor son and investment banker sons have helped with health and money. Our daughter with tutoring super-powers offered to homeschool our Native American daughter for a year and did so successfully.

We have another daughter who bakes us more delicious food than we can eat. Our artist daughter has enriched our lives with her works. Our youngest daughter, with unusually high emotional intelligence, has blessed us with extra compassion. They all have other gifts too, of course. We all have a multitude of gifts. We can all fill in gaps for each other in our families.

We have done family bake sales to raise money for a few different causes, but recently I have thought about having a family cause—something that our family is known for supporting and raising money for. It might be the Rock n' Roll Running Series, Seattle edition. I have run two half marathons with this organization. A handful of years ago, Seattle Rock n' Roll partnered with St. Jude Children's Research Hospital.

Even though many of our kids are grown, they are frequently in and out of our home, and I still delegate. As I type this, one daughter just left to pick up groceries. Another is making smoothie bases for the week. This morning a third one vacuumed our car. A little from each one adds up to a lot for me. I also help them with many tasks. It's family!

FAMILY HISTORY

We know for sure that serving each other on earth builds families. But what about serving our families who have gone home to heaven? Latter-day Saints believe that our ancestors are aware of us and want to help us. As we take interest in them, they take even more of an interest in us and can help us.

It's likely that you know, or have heard about, an expert in family history. Maybe this person is your great-aunt or your cousin. Maybe he or she has shared with you incredible finds, amazing stories, and the sheer delight of the pursuit.

I have some family history expert friends. They have that certain look in their eye when they talk about genealogy. It's a knowing look. It's hard to explain, but I would imagine it's similar to the look that the children in *The Lion, the Witch, and the Wardrobe* had when they returned from Narnia. It's a quiet joy. They have seen the other side. In this case, we're talking about the other side of the veil. It's wondrous. They want to go back again and again and again.

I remember one of these friends talking about trips to the Family History Library in Salt Lake City years ago. She said that she kept an eye on the clock the whole day, savoring the search, and nearly resenting the time it took to go to lunch. Every hour was precious. Every minute represented another potential discovery.

For years I would listen to these stories with a mixture of awe and (internal) yawning. I was baffled. How could combing through ancient information bring them such happiness? Genealogy seemed complicated and dry. I reminded myself that I went to the temple. I was still helping people on the other side.

And yet, I still made the occasional effort, out of sheer desire to be obedient, to understand the process. My expert friend Annette and I spent time on this together. When we weren't distracted and laughing, I made some genealogical progress. When I asked my expert friend Cathi for some help, she gave me an entire notebook filled with work she had done on my family line. This was above and beyond. It inspired me to want to do more of my own research.

Then progress hit the fast track after I read a quote about how family history can build family relationships. It can not only "turn the hearts of the fathers to the children, and the hearts of the children to their fathers" (Malachi 4:6), but it can turn the hearts of all family members toward each other. I thought about my many non-member siblings. I thought about my great love for them and my desire to help them progress. I thought about how this pursuit might offer us a common interest and bring us even closer. That was it. I was now rushing to be deeply invested.

I sat down with Ancestry.com, without Annette, and started digging. Basically, I just poked around. It's an intuitive, user-friendly site. Like a child, I just clicked on things that looked interesting. I began to figure out more and more. My time with Annette had been well spent. I was launched. When I didn't know what to do next, I asked Google for answers.

As I kept doing this for a few days, something incredible happened. I felt that "Whoosh!" It was that excitement I had heard so much about. It was that hunger. It was the thrill of the chase. One day I pushed myself back from my computer screen and had a realization.

Logically, I knew our Heavenly Parents are perfect in everything. That perfection, I realized, included fun. They are perfect at having fun, in the purest and best ways. When doing genealogy, you are playing the role of detective. You are searching for treasures (in this case, relatives). You are rewarded with the thrill of discovery.

I took a deep breath. God could have set this all up so differently. He could have made genealogy beyond easy. But heaven wanted us to have fun in the process. Wow.

I'm having a blast. Genealogy is the best game ever. Plus, it's free on Ancestry.com with membership in the Church. And it's not just Ancestry. Church membership includes free membership on other family history sites, like Find My Past and My Heritage.

The two best parts about playing this game, of course, are (1) ancestors are recognized and engaged; helping them helps them help us and (2) we become closer as a family as we work on our common mission to learn about our family members.

One of my sisters is now also caught up in the spirit of Elijah. We are both so deep into this detective game that we have new nicknames for each other based on the names of sister detectives from *The Dana Girls* book series we read as children. We trade information, photos, and stories. This has been a huge source of joy for both of us. We are closer than ever.

We have been sharing our information with our other siblings via emails and text messages. Fascinating finds have sparked interest, and we're just getting started. We're sharing heritage. We're sharing joy. We're sharing fun.

Are you looking for more true fun in your life? What if that fun also deeply blessed your ancestors? What if that fun helped you feel closer to your family? What if that fun also helped you avoid temptation? Genealogy has our tickets to ride. Heaven's got game! And this game is a game changer for good.

It's likely true that the first thing most people think of when they think of the Latter-day Saints is family. But the second thing is most likely service. From Mormon Helping Hands to missionaries serving humanitarian missions all over the world to your run-of-the-mill helpful Latter-day Saint neighbor, the Saints are known for serving. Latter-day Saint Charities tends to be quiet about all that it does. But since 1985, Latter-day Saint Charities has given 2.7 billion dollars to 197 countries in need.[6]

On a family scale, serving one another is also what the Saints, and so many others, believe the Lord would have us do. The infamous third little pig built his house out of bricks. Bricks are known for strength and endurance. When we build our homes with bricks of pure loving service, they will endure forever.

NUTS AND BOLTS

- The Saints believe that when we are serving one another, we are serving God.
- Serving one another is a major Latter-day Saint focus. It is considered, as the quote states, "the only door out of the prison of oneself." It helps us to overcome "the natural man." It is a major ingredient in any recipe for happiness.
- Delegation is key to helping children learn to serve and to greater parental freedom.
- Lavish praise helps all good behaviors (including those related to chores) to increase.
- In quiet teaching moments, teach children that happiness increases after chores are done and that there would be far

less happiness if there were no chores. This is because it is the contrast between the hard work and then the play that brings fulfillment.

- Pay attention to each child's unique gifts that can be employed in service.
- As we become more aware of our ancestors through family history, the Saints believe that those ancestors can then better serve us from the other side. Blessings will increase!

NOTES

1. Jana Stanfield, "All the Good," *Jana Stanfield*, September 18, 2014. https://www.janastanfield.com/2014/09/all-the-good/.
2. *Guide to the Scriptures*, "Natural Man"; scriptures.lds.org.
3. "When We're Helping," *Children's Songbook*, 198.
4. Joy Allison, "Which Loved Best?" *Poetry Nook*. Accessed November 28, 2021; https://www.poetrynook.com/poem/which-loved-best.
5. Whitney Archibald, "Homework," *Y Magazine*. Brigham Young University, November 5, 2021. https://magazine.byu.edu/article/homework.
6. "Latter-Day Saint Charities Boosts Global Efforts in 2020," *LDS Church News*, March 26, 2021; https://newsroom.churchofjesuschrist.org/article/latter-day-saint-charities-boosts-global-efforts-2020.

Chapter Four

Building Virtue

*All the gold which is under or upon the earth
is not enough to give in exchange for virtue.*[1]
—Plato

* * *

The object of mortality is to become increasingly pure.[2]
—Sheri Dew

**In our quest to build a stronger home, virtue switches on all the
lights. When family lights shine, the whole world is brighter.**
One day, when I was a freshly minted mom of a freshly minted teenage boy, I walked past a lingerie store. In the mammoth window
there was an only slightly less mammoth, extremely inappropriate
image. I looked around at people passing. Some of them were teenage boys. I thought of my own teenage boy. There was no way this
kind of advertising was a good idea. I decided to be brave and talk
to the clerk about it.

Inhaling deeply, I walked into the store. I tried to be light-
hearted. I greeted the clerk and suggested that maybe the window

advertisement could use a sweater or something. I don't remember exactly what I said. I was so nervous. To my surprise, the retail clerk was also nervous. I sensed she knew the window image was wrong, but she didn't know what to do. She looked down at the floor and mumbled vague words of agreement. She would "see what she could do." She "would let people know." I found myself looking down at the floor too, mumbling vagaries.

There we were, two sad women in need of an Oprah. Why Oprah, you may ask? This experience happened before Oprah's Golden Globe speech during the #MeToo movement. It was Tarana Burke who kicked off the #MeToo societal movement, but Oprah ran with the ball. Around the time of Oprah's speech, our nation began having conversations about appropriate boundaries like never before. About this same time, one night I walked into a new, swanky, mostly Millennials kind of establishment to pick up a pizza. The restaurant was packed. The vibe was "happening." The architecture was hip, rad, and whatever buzz words Millennials are using now (best guess: not the ones I just used).

The pizza box was a surprise. I had never seen such an odd, extremely inappropriate graphic on a pizza box. Could this happen with pizza? I mean, it was pizza. Still, there it was. There I was. I couldn't not say something to the waitress who handed me the box. I nodded toward it and said quietly: "Oprah said it was 'our time,' right? I mean, are we really going to stand by and let this kind of 'buy-in' to the sexual harassment agenda thing still happen in this post #MeToo movement era?" It was, decidedly, a lot of syllables leaving my mouth. But Oprah had stoked my fire.

The waitress's smile turned fierce. "Oh, yes! I hear you. A number of us have talked to them." She glanced behind her at management people. "These boxes are on their way out!" A nearby co-worker nodded in agreement. They looked at those boxes with a gaze typically reserved for someone trying to light up a cigarette on an airplane. Hoo. Ray. We had our Oprah moment. Hopefully, our nation will have many more.

"Sharks" of immorality and gratuitous violence are always waiting, just beneath the surface of many media channels, to reach out and take hold. With the explosion of the internet, there are more sharks than ever before in history. If my grandmother was right years ago when she said that "the world is going to hell in a handbasket," it does seem that the handbasket has picked up some speed recently.

I wonder what an "urban," contemporary version of Susanna Wesley, mother of the famous 1800s theologian John Wesley, might say. She once penned this famous quote: "Whatever weakens your reason, impairs the tenderness of your conscience, obscures your sense of God, takes off your relish for spiritual things, whatever increases the authority of the body over the mind, that thing is sin to you, however innocent it may seem in itself."[3]

Maybe the "hip" edition of Ms. Wesley would say, "Yeah, well, what I said then had some street cred back there in the 1800s, but now with all the garbage coming in through devices and stuff? Looks like y'all are busted."

But, of course, she wouldn't really say this. She was British. She would tell us to never, *never* give up. Then she would apologize for plagiarizing Winston Churchill. She was a good woman. There has been an abundance of tremendous, valiant men and women throughout history. They have stood as beacons of light in a shadowy world.

One of these men was Paul from the Old Testament. Joseph Smith quotes beloved Paul in the thirteenth Article of Faith: "We believe in being honest, true, chaste, benevolent, virtuous, and in doing good to all men; indeed, we may say that we follow the admonition of Paul—We believe all things, we hope all things, we have endured many things, and hope to be able to endure all things."

I love the word *virtuous* in Paul's admonition. Virtue is stealth power. You don't see it coming. But it works a treat, as the British might say.

The best thing about virtue is that it is far more powerful than we might guess. Virtue may appear "demure," but it's actually a force. It's your packing CIA grandmother serving up a basket of fresh rolls. There is more going on than meets the eye.

A scripture in the New Testament illustrates this:

And a woman having an issue of blood twelve years, which had spent all her living upon physicians, neither could be healed of any, came behind him, and touched the border of his garment: and immediately her issue of blood stanched. And Jesus said, Who touched me? When all denied, Peter and they that were with him said, Master, the multitude throng thee and press thee, and sayest thou, Who touched me?

And Jesus said Somebody hath touched me: for I perceive that virtue is gone out of me. And when the woman saw that she was not hid, she came trembling and falling down before him, she declared unto him before all the people for what cause she had touched him, and how she was healed immediately. And he said unto her, Daughter, be of good comfort: thy faith hath made thee whole; go in peace. (Luke 8:43–48)

Isn't it interesting that Jesus said, "Virtue is gone out of me"? Virtue healed the woman. Isn't that exciting? Virtue is powerful. It can heal. It can bless. It can make whole. Since everything has an opposite, we know what a lack of virtue can do. It can make us spiritually ill, it can curse, it can tear apart. The truth is that virtue really matters, so the adversary promotes the opposite message: that virtue doesn't really matter.

Historically, this pattern doesn't end well. Isaiah wrote, "Woe unto them that call evil good, and good evil; that put darkness for light, and light for darkness; that put bitter for sweet, and sweet for bitter!" (Isaiah 5:20).

We see this pattern in the media. You've noticed that media isn't always courting virtue. In fact, media rarely even uses the word *virtue*. Outside of a religious context, or our discussion here, when is the last time you heard the word *virtue*? 1843? I'm exaggerating of course, but it's not really a buzzword. For many, it's a Jane Austen sort of word. Or it could be a girl's name if you are a pilgrim. It can seem old-fashioned, out of date. Many seem to have grown tired of virtue, but this is like growing tired of the warmth of the sun. When society loses this warmth, the love of men waxes cold.

Isaiah wrote about this: "And because iniquity shall abound, the love of many shall wax cold" (Isaiah 24:12). Coldness and chaos often correlate with an absence of virtue. On the other hand, warmth, comfort, and peace all seem to correlate with the presence of virtue.

There is a particularly overlooked quality that correlates with virtue: confidence. This is such a fascinating concept.

It turns out that confidence doesn't come from a store. Perhaps it comes from something much more. (Thank you, Grinch). But seriously, *authentic self-confidence comes from virtue.*

Let's look at this scripture: "Let thy bowels also be full of charity towards all men . . . and let virtue garnish thy thoughts unceasingly; then shall thy confidence wax strong in the presence of God" (D&C 121:45). Following the logic here, *if our confidence can be strong in God's presence, is there any mere mortal who can then shake our confidence?*

So, following the D&C 121:45 recipe above, ipso facto, we know that the optimal combination for creating authentic confidence in ourselves is charity[4] (the pure love of Christ) garnished with virtue. This is true personal power.

Isn't that interesting? How many thousands of books have been written on how to have more confidence, more personal power? Methods presented may only skim the surface of the confidence issue, delivering results that may not feel fully authentic or sustainable.

The Savior cuts right to the heart of the matter with simple truth. He is the ultimate example of genuine personal power and confidence. He perfectly embodies the equation that perfect charity plus perfect virtue equals ultimate pure power.

We, as mortals, are not perfect, of course, and we will not be perfect on Earth as He was. But, we can increase our confidence and personal power by following our Savior and filling our souls with virtue and its companion, light.

I love this scripture: "And if your eye be single to my glory, your whole bodies shall be filled with *light*, and there shall be no darkness in you; and that body which is filled with *light* comprehendeth all things" (D&C 88:67; emphasis added).

We can shine that light brightly in our homes. We can shine it in the world. We can enjoy the sweet glow of authentic and humble self-confidence. We can radiate that glow. Our family can bask in its warmth. Our example will help them seek to create their own brighter lights.

We can do this no matter our personality type. My soft-spoken mom is so non-confrontational that she once took a class called "Assertiveness Training." But she could be brave—very brave—when it came to children.

I recall as a child being in a movie theatre one afternoon when the seemingly clean movie suddenly took a dark turn. My mom got up, gently took my hand, and began to guide me out of the theatre. On her way out she stopped, kneeled down in front of a couple with children, and told them they should leave. "Your children should not see this," she said kindly but firmly. The parents with whom she spoke did not react well. They were not kind to my mother. We left. I never forgot her example.

On another occasion during my childhood, my small siblings and I were gathered around a television set. We had been watching a children's show, but one of us had turned the channel, and suddenly, we were not watching *The Jetsons* anymore. The show was inappropriate. Mom walked in the room, saw what we were watching, and turned it off. She looked nervous as she surveyed us.

She cleared her throat and essentially said to her tiny bunch of fans, "We don't want to watch that. Marriage is beautiful and . . . important! This show doesn't understand that. This show is mocking marriage, so we don't want to watch this."

I was so young, and I had only the vaguest idea about what she was talking about. But she was earnest. That made an impression on preschool me. Marriage was a big deal. Teasing about marriage was also a big deal. Noted.

Looking back, I loved that my shy mom was willing to bumble through awkward words because she wanted to protect future us. She was brave and gently bold. You could almost hear angels softly applauding.

My father was also intelligent about media choices. He didn't tell off-color jokes or watch lewd media. He told us, his daughters, that he fell in love with our mom, in large part, *because* of her purity.

What a great thing for dads to share with their daughters! I am reminded of a story about Muhammad Ali. It took place when his daughters came to his home wearing clothes that were very revealing. His daughter shared:

> When we finally arrived, the chauffeur escorted my younger sister, Laila, and me up to my father's suite. As usual, he was hiding behind the door waiting to scare us. We exchanged many hugs and kisses as we could possibly give in one day.
>
> My father took a good look at us. Then he sat me down on his lap and said something that I will never forget. He looked me straight in the eyes and said, "Hana, everything that God made valuable in the world is covered and hard to get to. Where do you find diamonds? Deep down in the ground, covered and protected. Where do you find pearls? Deep down at the bottom of the ocean, covered up and protected in a beautiful shell. Where do you find gold? Way down in the mine, covered over with layers and layers of rock. You've got to work hard to get to them."
>
> He looked at me with serious eyes. "Your body is sacred. You're far more precious than diamonds and pearls, and you should be covered too."[5]

Thanks, Mr. Ali. Modesty is an even tougher issue today than when you gave those pearls of wisdom to your daughters. But we signed up for this earthly gig, right? We're on a field trip from our heavenly home. We're on a fact-finding mission. We are learning what truly brings long term joy and what is mirage.

This is challenging, of course, because "inflammatory media" is everywhere. Just as inflammatory (junk) food can poison our gut cells, inflammatory media can poison our minds.

How can we teach our children truths we have learned about embracing purity and eschewing that which is tainted? We can pray. We can watch for "teaching moments" and pray that our words will be seasoned with that optimal blend of conviction and kindness, sprinkled with boldness.

It is easier for me to teach when I remember my vision for motherhood and family and keep my potential influence in mind. I remind myself of quotes like this from James E. Faust: "There is no greater good in all the world than motherhood. The influence of a mother in the lives of her children is beyond calculation." [6]

Quotes like that remind me that I wear the invisible crown and the cape. We moms have superpowers. We need these, especially when it seems like celebrities are standing at the gates of the "large and spacious building," [7] trying to wave our children in.

We may want to say, "Hey there, hang on! Did you not know that some of us have been trying to raise our children on basically healthy foods and the philosophies of Mister Rogers? Why are you trying to mess with the wholesome purity we've been trying to spoon feed our offspring since birth?"

As long as there are watchful, good parents, the devil may care. We are his biggest threat. We are so much more powerful than we sometimes give ourselves credit for. When it comes to media, we can teach our children about the polar opposite feelings from the Holy Ghost (which witnesses that something is true) and the Media Monster (which feels oddly uncomfortable but may also arouse curiosity). The latter is a warning, indicating danger ahead. It's the feeling that lets you know it's time to turn the media off immediately. It's a warning directly from heaven.

Deep down we sense that power. We need that power today more than ever because the monsters we are battling are scarier than ever.

Enter one of the biggest monsters of all.

PORNOGRAPHY

To indulge in pornography leads to difficulties, divorce, disease, and troubles of a dozen kinds. There is no part of it that is innocent. To collect it, view it, or carry it around in any form is akin to keeping a rattlesnake in your backpack. It exposes you to the inevitable spiritual equivalent of the serpent's strike with its injection of deadly venom. [8]

—Boyd K. Packer

Satan has become a master at using the addictive power of pornography to limit individual capacity to be led by the Spirit. The onslaught of pornography in all of its vicious, corroding, destructive forms has caused great grief, suffering, heartache, and destroyed marriages. It is one of the most damning influences on earth. Whether it be through the printed page, movies, television, obscene lyrics, vulgarities on the telephone, or flickering personal computer screen, pornography is overpoweringly addictive and severely damaging.[9]
—Richard G. Scott

Pornography was developed by the adversary as a weapon of mass family destruction. It can create soul-crushing addictions for mostly men. For women, distorted images of sexuality can not only lead to addiction but more often to body dysmorphia and horrific eating disorders. Pornography can also lead to child abuse. It is insidious, terrifying, and dehumanizing.

When I think of the term "dehumanizing," I think of those who have created wars. One of their goals is to dehumanize the enemy so they are easier to destroy. The adversary wants to dehumanize the sexual experience—something that is, in reality, so glorious and powerful that it can spark human life. There is much science on pornography that is compelling.

For example, recently Mark Butler (Professor, School of Family Life, BYU) said:

> We're all familiar with popular portrayals of no-strings-attached sex—for example, the sitcom with a new paramour almost every episode. But human sexual systems don't actually work that way. And there are sound evolutionary reasons why.
>
> For starters, humans have relatively large brains. This is a significant evolutionary advantage, but to fully leverage those brains, humans require a much longer period of dependency for development.
>
> A strong maternal-child bond, or attachment, supports this extended development. That bond is most solid when

complemented by a strong relationship between father and mother as well as father and child. In other words, reciprocal familial bonds in all directions undergird the long-term developmental processes that foster a child's well-being. So, what does this have to do with pornography? Well, natural sexual reward systems promote attachments that are essential to fortifying these bonds. Pornography, however, short circuits these systems, distorting the processes and sexual scripts most helpful fostering the kind of attachment that supports long-term development and well-being.

Thus, sexual strategies that focus narrowly on maximizing short-term pleasure with few "strings attached," are actually not in the end as beneficial, speaking evolutionarily. For the overall well-being of parents and children, evolution-designed sex has lots of strings attached, weaving threads of couple attachment that keep their children safe and secure. They create pair-bonding that supports family life. Sex, in other words, promotes adult partners' and their children's well-being when embedded in long-term committed relationships in bonds of love and reciprocity.

Pornography, on the other hand, tends to teach young people and adults anti-attachment sexual scripts. More often than not, porn emphasizes noncommittal pleasure, sometimes at the expense of behaviors that do in fact lead to pair-bonding. Pornographic images and narratives are at odds with the natural attachment functions of human sexual systems. And, as such, pornography may have consequences for how emerging adults choose to approach sex and relationships.

For example, in a recent analysis, a team of scholars analyzed 40 years of research pertaining to pornography and impersonal sex and found that "pornography consumption was a robust predictor of both impersonal sexual attitudes and impersonal sexual behavior."

In other words, pornography is most often anti-attachment, portraying sex as uncommitted physical gratification. This in turn can influence the sexual attitudes, behaviors and norms surrounding our most intimate relationships, usually to the detriment of critical familial relationships.[10]

Pornography is a perverted and deeply broken version of what intimacy can be. But this broken thing doesn't have to break us. We can arm ourselves with information and faith. We can pray to receive the revelation and learning we need to deal with this media shark of our day.

Sensing what might be coming, my husband and I intentionally raised our kids with very little TV. We were really careful about movies. When our kids asked to watch a questionable movie, we would ask them to go to the website Kids in Mind and read the movie description to us out loud.

If the movie was sketchy, the description was likely to be very embarrassing to read out loud. Our children didn't even want to finish reading the description and would awkwardly bow out of wanting to see the film. Every time, this would save the day.

What will save us from this global morality pandemic? There are so many mixed messages today. People are encouraged to stay away from this drug of pornography, but then "dealers" show up on television and phones. When young girls see their role models with stripper poles and inappropriate clothing, they absorb the carefully chosen subtext: "Men have the power. You want to get along in this world? Focus on sex. Let yourself be manipulated, used, and disempowered." Then people wonder why so many women have eating disorders, why so many men have soul-crushing pornography addictions, why children are sexually abused, and why sex trafficking just keeps getting worse.

Physical intimacy, in the right setting, is awesome. There is a time and a place for all of these feelings and the expressions of them. God gave us sexual intimacy to enjoy and treasure.

But there is a reason it's called "intimacy." It's intimate, private, beautiful, and even sacred. I'm not saying we need to turn over any TV tables. But we can definitely turn off the TV and other screens. We can turn away from half-truth cocktails laced with soul poison. We can take stands in our homes and communities. We can listen to that still small voice inside of each of us. It knows the way, and the way to get away.

We are a better country than this. America was not founded on weakness. The Pilgrims were not wimps. Our Revolutionary forefathers were not spineless. Our immigrants, whom we welcomed to Ellis Island, were not lacking in grit and determination. We need that bravery, that fortitude, and that courage again. And we need bravery beyond our borders. We need "virtue bravery" all over the world. As in the Hans Christian Andersen tale, we need to stand up to "emperors," our societies, and declare that way too many people are not wearing enough, or any, clothing.

We were built on integrity, decency, and morality. Our ancestors, many of whom gave up everything to advance what are now our current situations, are still watching us. Can we show our thanks by increasing our grit, determination, and decency? We can!

If there is one thing I wish we could teach all children and young adults it is this: when your spirit feels uncomfortable about something, if it feels "off"; if it feels unsafe and/or you feel uncomfortable in your spirit, remove yourself from the situation immediately.

We have to learn to recognize this feeling of discomfort and know when to run. We can't wait until kids are teenagers to teach them about this. When they are very young they need to learn to recognize the difference between feelings coming from the Holy Ghost and those from the adversary. When those feelings come from the adversary, they need to know to *run*.

Think of Joseph and Potiphar's wife. Think of burning buildings. They need to get away fast. Their souls and future happiness need them to go, and go immediately. They can learn that that sinking/strange curiosity arousing feeling inside them when they view something inappropriate is a warning from heaven.

Sixteen states now call pornography a public health crisis.[11] Pornography is family poison. Bishops and pastors have said that pornography is the number-one thing that boys come to access help with as they try to move past it. They come broken and emotional. They often say it started with unfortunate media choices that are accepted, even applauded in the world. These choices are "gateway drugs." Parents today need to be gatekeepers.

THE GOOD STUFF

We've talked about awful things we forever want to avoid. Now, let's talk about good stuff we want our family to embrace. Latter-day Saints love this quote by Biblical Paul. It's even in one of their articles of faith: "If there is anything virtuous, lovely, or of good report or praiseworthy, we *seek* after these things" (Articles of Faith 1:13; emphasis added). Don't you love the word *seek* in this passage? I have an inner Nancy Drew that loves the idea of searching, carefully observing, and seeking after things that are virtuous, lovely, of good report, and praiseworthy. They are all around us, "hidden in plain sight." The search can be part of the fun.

One of my husband's and my favorite things in life is listening to our children discuss praiseworthy media that they all love. These discussions are endlessly fun. They are also seemingly endless. I am thrilled because I hope they will continue to have fun discussions about things of "good report" forever.

Often, one of them will find something delightful. Then they will share it with their siblings and Tom and me, and it will catch fire. *Avatar, the Last Airbender,* is a great example of this. I think all of them have watched every episode more than once. Spouses have joined the fun. The discussions about this show are as delightful (for me, more delightful) than the actual show. There is something about the clever elixir of ensemble comedy blended with the vulnerability and passion of Aang (the main character) and the ancient setting that just nails it in the innocent fun department. Did I mention it's animated? In this case, that just adds to the fun for all ages.

Another classic series, of course, is *Star Wars*. Maybe the whole world bonds over this one. I think we are all drawn to *Star Wars* in part because the overarching "journey" theme is reflective of our own journey as we travel through mortality. We, too, are in a new realm. We, too, are facing good and evil every day. We, too, are vulnerable and often reluctant heroes. We, too, love family and have a lot to figure out there. We, too, look for a "force" greater than our own. A co-producer for the original *Star Wars* was Gary Kurtz, who is a Latter-day Saint.

The Lord of the Rings also fits in this "good versus evil" category. The list goes on.

My daughters and I bond over Hallmark Christmas movies, munching on snacks and bundling up in blankets as we watch. The plots are often marshmallow fluff, and part of the fun is joking about the Hallmark movie formula while we watch. It's all pretty meta, but we genuinely adore the refreshing innocence of these romances. We also love the sets. Well done, Hallmark!

We are also fans of the sports movie genre. This surprises me because I am not usually drawn to sports. As it turns out, there are many smart, clean plots in this genre. Have you seen *The Blindside*? Or *Cool Runnings*? Or *Remember the Titans*? What about *Miracle*, or our favorite in this category, *The Sandlot*? We have oft quoted the line "You're killing me, Smalls" to each other in conversations. We quote many good movies. Quoting movie lines has given us inside jokes that are bonding.

We also love a number of classic movies that we watch over and over as a family. This is a short list of movies that will appeal to differing age levels:

- *Singing in the Rain* (our number-one favorite family film)
- *Random Harvest*
- *Mr. Smith Goes to Washington*
- *The Three Musketeers* (with Gene Kelly)
- *Robin Hood* (with Errol Flynn)
- *The Glenn Miller Story* (with Jimmy Stewart and June Allyson)
- *The Sound of Music* (a particular favorite of Tom's)
- *Heidi* (With Shirley Temple. This one can break your heart in a good way. The book is more spiritual and a great testimony-builder of Christ for children.)
- *My Fair Lady*
- *The Hundred-Foot Journey*
- *The Finest Hours* (The acting is incredible.)
- *Newsies*
- *Empire of the Sun*
- *The Bluebird* (With Shirley Temple. This movie has a reference to premortality.)

- *Soul* (This recent movie also references the idea of a premortal world. It's animated and takes lots of flights of fancy, but it's fun.)
- *Seven Brides for Seven Brothers* (another family favorite)
- *Little Women* (There are a lot of versions, and they just keep getting better!)
- *Coco* (great movie that emphasizes the importance of family)
- *Cars*
- *MegaMind*
- *Inside Out* (a great jumping off point for talking about feelings)
- *Moana* (More realistic body types are a plus.)
- *The Incredibles* (strong on family)
- *Brave*
- *Cinderella*
- *Snow White*
- *Beauty and the Beast*
- *Ever After* (with Drew Barrymore)
- *Sleeping Beauty*
- *Cinderella,* live action (We can't say enough good things about this movie.)

The Chosen is a TV series in a class by itself. A collaborative effort between Evangelicals, Jews, and Latter-day Saints, this one might knock your spiritual socks off.

Family Ties is a television show that was filmed in the 1980s. It's all about family, in so many wonderful ways. Even the opening song about family has brought tears to my eyes. Here are a couple of lines from that song. "And there ain't no nothin' we can't love each other through . . . What would we do, baby, without us?" The breakout star of this show is a young Michael J. Fox. He is outstanding, as is the whole cast. The show is funny, even when sometimes addressing serious topics that families may experience. So many shows are not worth our time. This one is.

Christmas movies can bring good feelings year around. *White Christmas, Miracle on 34th Street, A Charlie Brown Christmas,* and

It's a Wonderful Life, which will remind you and yours that our mortal experience is actually wonderful, are all great choices.

The BYU (Latter-day Saint affiliation) TV channel is so clean you could leave it on all day and never wonder if your children were getting exposed to untoward things. One of their best shows is *Studio C.* It's a sketch comedy show, and many of the sketches are hilarious. Not all of them "land," however, so I have done meticulous (and fun) research for you. See my *HuffPost* article, "Parenting Hack: Use Clean Comedy to Bond With Your Kids" to find links for some of the *Studio C* sketches that are particularly funny (April 26, 2017; available at https://www.huffpost.com/entry/parenting-hack-use-clean-comedy-to-bond-with-your_b_58ea6c1fe4b0acd784ca5983).

Literature can be another fantastic family bonding experience that brings all the warm and fuzzy feels. It starts with reading to very young children. Reading a wonderful book to a little child or children is one of the most sublime things I have ever experienced in mortality. I'm not exaggerating. There is a tender, pure spirit there that is incomparable. Our family has read so many delightful children's books through the years, over and over:

- *Blueberries for Sal*
- The *Francis* series
- *The Tales of Oliver and Amanda Pig*
- *The Velveteen Rabbit*
- *Love You Forever*
- *Heidi*
- *Charlotte's Web*
- *The Trumpet of the Swan*
- Anything written by Sandra Boynton

And dozens upon dozens more. There are, of course, other incredible books that have come out since our children were young:

- *Extra Yarn* by Mac Barnett
- *Chirri & Chirra* by Kaya Doi
- *Not Quite Snow White* by Ashley Franklin
- *Just Add Glitter* by Angela DiTerlizzi

- *Little Elliot, Big City* by Mike Curato
- *Last Stop on Market Street* by Matt de la Pena and Christian Robinson
- *Jabari Jumps* by Gaia Cornwall
- *This Is Not My Hat* by Jon Klassen
- *Dragons Love Tacos* by Adam Rubin
- *Not Quite Narwal* by Jessie Sima

These suggestions are the tip of the "delightful books for children" iceberg. There are so many, and it's so much fun to read them to little people. We have started something called "Sunday Stories" on Zoom. Every possible Sunday, I read to my grandchildren on Zoom. Then I send the recording to our various families (even the ones in our neighborhood) so that the children can watch these again. Last week we read *The Velveteen Rabbit*. It brought tears to my eyes and mostly riveted attention from our preschoolers. Sometimes they have questions, so they raise their hands over Zoom. We always happily stop for questions. Memories made!

For older kids, Brandon Sanderson has written many favored books. Diana Wynn Jones, C. S. Lewis (author of *The Chronicles of Narnia*), Rick Riordan, Megan Whalen Turner, and *Holes* author Louis Sachar are also beloved among our children. Of course, likely no one can forget J. K. Rowling, author of the *Harry Potter* series.

POSSIBLY THE MOST CRITICAL THING

One of the most important gifts you can ever give your child is the gift of standing firm, whilst being kind, when you don't give them a cell phone until they are older teenagers. It's guaranteed that they will ask for a phone sooner. By standing kindly strong on this you are saving them from years of "Pandora's box" phone addiction and subsequent misery.

The other critical gift is to protect available devices like computers and those eventual phones. We have a loved one whose parents were militant about protecting devices while all of the kids in the family were growing up. The kids were sometimes angry with their parents about this, but the parents did not respond with contention. Nor did they change their minds.

Our loved one told us that in later years every single child, unprompted and alone (without knowing their siblings were doing the same thing), went to their parents and thanked them profusely. None of them had pornography or phone addictions, but they could see many of their friends suffering with those things. Be strong. Stay strong. You can have a little hard now or possibly a lot of hard later.

NUTS & BOLTS

- Virtue is *a literal power*. Jesus used His own virtue to heal people.
- Be brave about standing up for virtue. Your children are taking mental notes. They will follow your lead.
- Teach children to recognize the difference between things that encourage good feelings and those which make us feel "off" and uncomfortable.
- Teach them, "If it feels off, run off." Leave the computer and/or environment immediately. Tell a parent or trusted adult.
- Keep your home as free from unclean media as possible. Create strong, clear boundaries.
- A pure home helps to create a safe, secure environment where children can enjoy trust and comfort. In such an environment they can grow to be their best selves.
- Teach them to love books more than media. Reading with small children creates forever bonds.
- Teach them the story of Queen Esther, and help them to realize that they "may have come to the earth for such a time as this" (Esther 4:14). They have.
- *Wait as long as possible* to give them media devices. We have a sixteen-year-old who still doesn't have a phone. She is happy. Phones can be a breeding ground for pornography.

When/if you get them devices, *figure out protection strategies* as soon as possible.

• Remember Paul's teaching, "If there is anything *virtuous, lovely, or of good report or praiseworthy, we seek after these things.*"

NOTES

1. Plato, "Laws, by Plato," Project Gutenberg, October 20, 2008. https://www.gutenberg.org/files/1750/1750-h/1750-h.htm.

2. Sheri L. Dew, *No One Can Take Your Place* (Salt Lake City, UT: Deseret Book, 2004), 19.

3. John Whitehead, *The Life of the Rev. John Wesley* (Madison, WI: The University of Wisconsin–Madison, 1846), 239.

4. Gospel Topics, "Charity," https://www.churchofjesuschrist.org/study/manual/gospel-topics/charity.

5. Hana Ali, *More Than a Hero: Muhammad Ali's Life Lessons Presented Through His Daughter's Eyes* (United Kingdom: Hodder & Stoughton, 2001).

6. James E. Faust, "Fathers, Mothers, Marriage," *Ensign or Liahona*, August 2004, 3.

7. BMC TEAM, "What Is the Significance of the Great and Spacious Building?" *Book of Mormon Central*, January 17, 2020; https://knowhy.bookofmormoncentral.org/knowhy/what-is-the-significance-of-the-great-and-spacious-building.

8. Boyd K. Packer, "Truths Worth Knowing," *Ensign or Liahona*, August 2014, 49.

9. Richard G. Scott, "To Acquire Spiritual Guidance," *Ensign or Liahona*, November 2009, 8.

10. Mark Butler, Hal Boyd, and Kaylin Cash, "Don't Let a Pornography Boom Disrupt Human Attachment," *Deseret News*, September 18, 2020; https://www.deseret.com/opinion/2020/9/18/21440005/guest-opinion-pornography-boom-human-attachment-isolation-covid-19-pandemic.

11. Fight the New Drug Editorial Team, "These 16 U.S. States Passed Resolutions Recognizing Porn as a Public Health Issue," *Fight the New Drug*, November 20, 2020; https://fightthenewdrug.org/here-are-the-states-that-have-passed-resolutions/.

Chapter Five

Building Routines

We are what we repeatedly do. Excellence, then,
is not an act, but a habit.[1]
—Aristotle

* * *

The secret of your future is hidden
in your daily routine.[2]
—Mike Murdock

Routines are the fences around our strong homes. They engender feelings of safety, security, and comfort. The Saints, like many others, believe that God loves structure. They believe in modern scriptures on this topic, such as, "For God is not a God of confusion but peace" (1 Corinthians 14:33) and "Organize yourselves; prepare every needful thing; and establish a house, even a house of prayer, a house of fasting, a house of faith, a house of learning, a house of glory, a house of order, a house of God" (D&C 88:119).

The second scripture pulled me up short as a non-member at BYU in my college days. I had never heard of it, but I had left some unwashed dishes in our apartment sink one day. That evening, this scripture was posted above the sink. Wow. These girls were too kind to call me out on my error. Instead, they just posted a principle. They were "saints" indeed!

Years ago, I winced as I ran across another structure scripture that read in part, "See that all these things are done in wisdom and order" (Mosiah 4:27). I was totally fine with the wisdom part, but order? You know from previous pages of this book that order was a sticky wicket for me. When you are naturally spontaneous, the idea of orderly routines can feel constricting. It's like wanting to wear a loose, flowy dress, but someone hands you a too-tight jacket instead.

Over time, I've learned to love that jacket. I've learned to make it fit fairly well. It's not a perfect fit, and I am far from perfect, but I've learned that basic order is a gift that makes so many other gifts easier in families. One of those gifts is a sense of calm. Even very basic, imperfect order offers this gift. It's a gift that keeps on giving.

David Code, author of *Kids Pick up on Everything: How Parental Stress Is Toxic to Kids*, said, "My goal with my kids is not to tell them I love them every six minutes of the day and helicopter-parent them so they know I'm present. It's to create calm around them so that they feel no sense of threat."[3]

We believe that our Heavenly Parents, just like our earthly parents, want us to keep our rooms clean. Calm environments, physically and emotionally, help us "feel no sense of threat." We believe that God wants peace, order, purity, and wisdom in our homes. Our homes are small units that make up the whole world. If all of our homes were peaceful, we could someday achieve that wish of seemingly every Miss USA candidate—world peace.

A path from chaos to peace travels through the land of routines. I've learned that routines give us more and less: less annoyance, less confusion, less wasted time. And more: more love, more confidence, more unruffled hours.

I love routines when I do them routinely. My problem is that (as mentioned above) I also love spontaneity. I used to think that routines and spontaneity were not compatible. I've since learned that regular routines make occasional spontaneity even more fun. This is because spontaneity can be fraught with fear if there is no undergirding life preparation. For example, we can take off for a last-minute, fun picnic if we are generally organized and mostly caught up on routines. Then we can easily afford to dip out for a bit. But if we are generally unorganized and far behind in our routines, we may not be able to have this spontaneity. To this end, I have memorized this Latter-day Saint scripture with some of the kids. "If you are prepared, ye shall not fear" (D&C 38:30). This scripture has seemingly endless applications, doesn't it?

To illustrate how frazzled life can be without routines, let's pop in the time machine to a time when routines were nary to be seen and the outcome was less than serene.

> 'Twas frazzled days before Christmas and all through the house
> Not a creature was cleaning, and I felt like a louse
> I hung my head in stressed-out despair,
> hoping the Merry Maids soon would appear
> The children weren't nestled in their unmade beds
> They were sneaking snacks in the pantry instead.

I am standing at the back of the high school gym, waiting for one of my sons' Christmas band concerts to begin. My arms are overflowing with sports forms due the next day. Why did children need to do sports anyways? (Darn child-labor laws—they ruined everything!)

Why was I filling out forms at a band concert? Because this band concert felt like the quieter, more together place at the moment.

"Please, please don't let anyone sit next to me," I plead silently. But LeeAnn does. Large hair, big smile, voluminous coat. She nearly vibrates with enthusiasm.

"Looks like you've got a lot goin' on there!" she says in a Texas drawl that is both slightly annoying and endearing. I don't look up from the paper pile. She continues, "That's our son up there on stage . . . third from the left. He's a tuba player."

I don't know any tuba players. What I do know is that I am never, ever going to be done with sports forms. I will die, and they will bury me with sports forms to complete in heaven.

"So, which one is yours?"

I scan the stage. Boys in nice suits, check. My son is in a nice suit, but where is he?

"I don't see him, but he's up there," I say determinedly, looking down again. *Concentrate, Mary.*

She nods cheerfully. "Well, it is pretty crowded up there. Which instrument does he play?"

Which . . . what? So sleep deprived . . . so bleary. Frantic deadlines . . . Why do I have to know which instrument he plays? Deep breath. This is ridiculous. I am his mother. Of course, I must know! Then, suddenly, I can picture the instrument in my head. I just can't for the life of me *say* it.

"Well," I say, trying to sound confident, yet casual, "you know those Christmas cards with the sweet little instruments on them? You know . . . often on a mantel or on a tree as an ornament?"

"The French horn?"

"Exactly!" I try to hide my panic under a thin veneer of false confidence. She looks at me with a raised eyebrow. She's skeptical but compassionate. It's like she's saying, "Do you need some time away on a beach, you brain-fogged-out mom?" Come to almost think clearly about it, I do. Is there anything sunshine and ocean sand can't improve?

But what I also needed was a return to the routines that had blown away in the whirlwind of our chaotic life. I needed those structured but flexible schedules that blessed our lives abundantly. Without them, I was living *reactively*, not *proactively*. I needed a clipboard and some plans, stat.

With basic time structure built into our family lives, we can be more flexible with greater ease. Think of the Brooklyn Bridge. Its strong structure is awesome, but it's also subtly flexible, right? It can move with shifts in the wind. It can handle whatever random weather blows its way.

We see this nod to flexibility in the movie *The Incredibles*. Remember Elastigirl's superpower? It's flexibility! Wasn't this a brilliant choice? Flexibility is the superpower all moms need, but especially moms of young children. If you are one of these moms, you know that I have the highest respect for you in a critically important job. The world may not tell you every day that you are amazing, but I want to keep on telling you because you are!

You know it can be challenging to create family routines because motherhood is different from the world of work or school. I understand. Not long after I became a mom, I chose to stay home full-time. I didn't know that I would feel lonely sometimes. I didn't know that I would feel a lack of structure, or that I would miss feeling validated. I had been in a school or work environment for so long. These venues were all about structure, validation, and rewards.

When I was in school, the world said, "Here are the hoops, jump through them." So I jumped, year after year. I received good grades. I had an academic scholarship in college. It was a system I understood. Success felt like mine for the taking. Full-time motherhood was different. There was no validation system in place, though my husband tried his best to notice the good when he got home each day. The usual concrete, tangible reward suspects felt vague and far away. You don't see results right away.

Of course, there were new and different rewards: the feeling of being needed more than ever before, the smiles and coos and snuggles. There was a sense of maternal fulfillment that now had a place for continual expression. There were endless opportunities for creativity and memory making.

It wasn't an easy adjustment, but it was doable. I missed the structure of my previous life, the easy contact with others. I could accept and initiate social invitations now, but this took a new type of effort. I was out of my comfort zone, and sometimes I felt a little lost. The key, I realized, was to create my own structure. Fortunately, children thrive on schedules. They were happiest when there were good answers to their daily question, "What are we going to do today, Mommy?" This is true whether you are working outside the home or not. Children just love to know what's next.

Being naturally spontaneous and tending to want to live in the moment, I've had to train myself to deeply consider future moments. It was hard for me to learn to plan for upcoming moments, hours, days, and months, but this process has gotten so much better over time.

One thing that has really helped is what I call "three days out." Although I try to plan for the week and month every Sunday evening,

I also try to keep the next three days on my continual mental radar. I try to use spare mental time to do this. You know those random minutes while waiting in line or what have you? I try to think, "What needs doing in the next three days?" Then I try to record that list on my phone, or I review what has already been recorded. Sometimes I even just repeat these items over and over in my mind, adding a mental list to the "hard drive" in my brain. This keeps me aware as I scan the mental horizon of three days ahead.

Sometimes I even imagine my closet and choose outfits in my mind so they are ready to go. I also picture the layout of Costco and mentally shop the aisles. I think about family members that need "something extra," some little bit of nurturing or help. I add that to the list. I plan meals three days out. This is incredibly helpful. I even try to see myself prepping and cooking in the kitchen. Rather than just waiting at, say, the post office, the brain can "see" the prepping steps and calculate approximate times needed. In my mind I can "look" in the fridge and calculate a shopping list with what I can recall is on hand. I miss a lot of things, but this process still blesses us. I love the saying, "My imperfect efforts bless my family perfectly."

Now I can plan some things a few weeks out at a time. The brain is incredibly powerful as we tap into its powers. On this domestic ship of life I am continually making tactical errors, but regular planning and routines have saved me from capsizing.

If you think about how important family life is to God, and to each of us, then it makes sense that the adversary would want to divert our attention away from its importance. He does this in two ways:

1. Encouraging us to devalue domestic efforts (personally and as a culture).
2. Making extra domestic efforts feel impossible—too Pinterest, too time consuming. The truth is that domestic efforts aren't everything, but they are something extraordinary. These efforts add dimension and color to the future memories of our children and to the memories of all those who spend time in our homes. A little time spent planning and

streamlining adds up to more time spent enjoying our families and all other aspects of our lives.

For example, I once read a book on home organization that spent an entire chapter on the value of doing *all* your laundry on one day. She convinced me! On the laundry room door I posted each family member's name and their assigned laundry day. All of their clean laundry needed to depart the room by the end of their individual days. This worked like a charm to keep our laundry room far neater and more organized. Routines for the win!

Daily routines start in the mornings, of course, and many of the Saints believe that morning is the best part of each day. I kind of think it may be God's favorite part of each day as well, but that is a topic for another article, or even another book.

MORNING GLORIES

If success is determined by high engagement, arousal and getting a lot done, larks have an advantage.[4]
—Glenn Brassington

Lose one hour in the morning and you'll spend all day looking for it.[5]
—Richard Whately

Latter-day Saints believe that the man upstairs is a morning person. They believe that He is the author of the Word of Wisdom, which says in part, "Cease to be idle; cease to be unclean; cease to find fault one with another; cease to sleep longer than is needful; *retire to thy bed early, that ye may not be weary; arise early, that your bodies and your minds may be invigorated*" (D&C 88:124; emphasis added).

Summer after summer, as my noisy teens and returning college kids would gather home, I would post this scripture on the refrigerator. Yet, sometimes they would stay up too late, laughing their heads off whilst chatting. Sometimes I was laughing with them. Still, we believe. We are trying! We have seen awesome results when we go to bed early and arise early. Our minds really are invigorated in the early mornings, once we get through the few minutes of "stumble bumble" (as my husband calls it) that waking up provides us. We really are less weary when we routinely go to bed early.

Since we are past the baby years, my husband and I are often in bed by nine or nine thirty p.m. and up by five or six a.m. I love mornings, once I am up and going, more than I can describe in earthly words. There is just this bliss, this reverential bliss, especially outside when the sun arrives. Have you felt this too?

What do Margaret Thatcher (former prime minister of Great Britain), Frank Lloyd Wright (architect), Robert Iger (CEO of Disney), Tim Cook (CEO of Apple), Leo Babauta (of Zen Habits), and Jack LaLanne (celebrated fitness expert) have in common? They arose/arise between four and five a.m. each day. They were/are true believers in the power of early mornings.

Jack LaLanne would apparently wake up and lift weights for ninety minutes. Then he would go for a swim or a run for thirty minutes. He did this routine for sixty years. The quality of his later years was magnificent compared to most. He lived to be ninety-six.

Getting up early (before, say, 6:30 a.m.) is for everyone. Little children seem to come from heaven wired for it. This practice is key to having a far less ruffled day. It's a secret of calm moms everywhere.

I remember when our first toddler toddled his way over to our bed unreasonably early in the morning. "Mommy!" he said, tugging on my blankets. "Time for bwekest (breakfast)!" *Oh my gosh,* I thought, squeezing my eyes tighter together in protest. *Where is the sleep love? Why aren't children issued nannies at birth? Why are our tax dollars going anywhere else?* I opened my eyes slightly.

There he was, with that mop of fluffy dark brown hair and wide melted-chocolate-chip brown eyes. He was so innocent. He was hungry. Of course, I got up and fed him. The next morning, the little life coach was back—a tiny Anthony Robbins, with a lisp. He made sure I was up and going. After a lot of this, I was trained.

There was no going back. Eventually, to my own surprise, I found myself getting up before him.

Early morning time is sacred to me now. I can't live without it. I feel cheated if I get up after six thirty a.m. The mental push to get up is worth it because of the joy I experience.

You know that feeling of childhood anticipation when you were so excited you could hardly stand it? Who knew that that feeling is available every early morning? Everything is ahead! Everything seems possible. And we've already experienced a victory—getting up. That feeling of success plus relished potential equals joy. It's possible to accomplish more before nine a.m. than many do in an entire day. That's invigorating!

This is especially true if the early morning includes walking or running. Henry David Thoreau nailed it when he said, "An early morning walk is a blessing for the whole day."[6] I just want to sing that from the rooftops. An early walk or run appears to be such a simple thing, but the implications are profound.

Even just a thirty-minute daily walk does the following:

- Speeds up the release of endorphins, which helps us to feel happy, even elated.
- Improves circulation, including circulation to the brain. Our minds become clearer and are able to think better.
- Improves digestion, which in turn seems to improve everything.
- Can reduce high blood pressure and high cholesterol.
- Can lower the risk of heart disease by 30 to 40 percent.
- Cuts the risk of stroke in half.
- Regularly strengthens bones and joints, and can help prevent osteoporosis.
- Is easier on joints than running.
- Is one of the best things you can do for your back, by promoting muscular development and increasing circulation.
- Increases oxygen intake, which then speeds up the fat-burning process.
- Blesses joints, opening some of the "chakras," or energy channels.

- Promotes better quality, deeper sleep.
- Boosts the immune system.
- Is better than medication for relieving symptoms of depression.[7]

All of these things translate into less stress, which can lead to more peace and positivity at home. You know the saying: "When Mama is happy, everyone is happy." It's time well invested.

Early morning glory is a daily prize not always easily won. Here is a winning and possible plan:

1. Wake up as early as it can work for you. Try to read/listen to something that feeds your soul.
2. Expect the wrestle. Wrestle with the wrestle. I (usually) win the wrestle. It's mind over mattress! In warmer months I listen for birds chirping out there, cheering me on.
3. I say "thank you" to the man upstairs. At any given time, there are innumerable things for which to be grateful, even on the hardest days.
4. Wrestle with the exercise *du jour*. I recognize that the temptation to avoid exercise is normal for me. I try to let the negative "Don't worry about exercising today" thoughts pass through my mind without giving them my attention. I don't try to argue. I just try to ignore them. The goal is to just keep moving toward . . . moving. Body peace and energy are around the corner.
5. Expect the unexpected. There may be missing items, unhappy children, and so on. I try to find, cheer, and do whatever else needs doing as quickly as I can. If you have young children, you could load them up in a double stroller/front pack. I load up grandchildren in a double stroller sometimes. I just did this today! I walk with daughters or friends or go solo with God and a good podcast. I just go, unless it's driving rain. Streaming workouts are everywhere now to complement your outside times. There is so much fun variety. Right now I am learning country dancing. A little research may reveal something you love. I also recommend *Trim Healthy Mama's*

Workins. These are two biological sisters who teach workouts together. They are a lot of fun.

6. Expect to possibly feel discomfort the first ten minutes or so of the walk/run/workout. The body is loosening up.

7. Enjoy! Happiness usually kicks in after the first ten or so minutes. Natural endorphins start to release. I am in an ever-increasingly good mood. The walk or run invites all the senses to the nature party. I call the endorphins "God-dor-phins." I believe that God made the gorgeous sky and trees and earth that we can see. God made the lovely floral scents that may envelop us. God made the warmth of the sun-shine that comforts us. God made tiny birds that cheerfully chirp, encouraging us on our journeys. When it's raining, I remember that He made the rain too. Walking in light rain has its own kind of beauty. I am not a fan of walking in driving rain.

Ideally, I like to be up for a while before anyone else in the house is up. When the kids were smaller, I just needed time to think clear, uninterrupted thoughts. I also needed to prepare for their arrival. Hosting small children is basically hosting adorable, funny, messy, and demanding guests at a year-round bed and breakfast. Being up before them helped tremendously.

Early morning is when the world is at its "Zen" peak. Once we are fully awake, we often feel settled, yet energized. Getting tasks out of the way early helps us to relax when the kids wake up. Instead of feeling run over by a herd of toddlers, we're ready for them. We're calm. It's okay if they are needing us and we're not getting a lot done because, after all, we just got a lot done.

Early morning action can set a calmer tone for the rest of the day. Besides, as a young mom, sometimes you just need some time alone. Why is early morning such a great time to get things going? Here's why:

• Studies show that our creative energy is highest then.[8]
• Studies indicate that our "willpower muscle" is strongest

early in the day.[9] Do we need to do something especially hard? Early morning is a great time to tackle it.

- If we can get dinner even partially prepared, we will have one less stress to worry about during the day.
- Early morning is a great time to think without distractions. It's a really sacred time. The mind is so fresh. It's an excellent time to make decisions.

PERKS FOR THE PERKY: MORE EARLY RISER BENEFITS

Early risers tend to earn significantly higher grades (per a 2008 study from the University of North Texas),[10] are more likely to anticipate problems and be proactive[11] (hugely helpful for moms), and give better job performance.[12] There is no more important job than motherhood.

What are some other great things to do when we're up early? Here are some proven ways to set a calm tone for the day:

- Drink a lot of water (at least sixteen ounces), preferably with lemon. Lemon is an internal detoxifier. Its citrusy tones also smell happy.
- Have a green smoothie.
- Put on a facial mask and enjoy its tightening and toning effects while you check your email, Facebook, and so on (and while sipping that water or a "hot lemon"—hot water with lemon and honey).

All of these things translate into less stress and more peace at home. Early morning exercise blesses the entire day.

Do you have a lark toddler or two who wants to be up when you are? I understand. I had several larks. I told these little friends that this was Mommy's quiet time to exercise and prepare for the day. My sister-in-law, of a similar bent, made a little "morning box" filled with activities for her early girl.

Sometimes if I was doing calisthenics, I would invite the toddlers to join me as "weights" on my legs, and I would lift them up and down. But mostly we kept to the quiet time rule. This was not only good for me, but I hope it was good modeling for their own future adult mornings.

Can having a daily quiet time for children help prevent anxiety in their later years? I believe so. Here's a testimonial of that: "As a kid, my mom would always make sure we had our 'quiet time' before we started the day. I kind of hated it, but as I get older, I still do it. It stuck with me, and I see the effects. People tell me that I am really cool all the time (which isn't true; who is cool all the time?). But I get what they mean. I take life *very* easy no matter what I may be going through. I attribute part of it to my quiet time."

The best mornings start with strong preparation. I learned this the hard way. I used to spend copious amounts of time trying to find the "morning things." But now I have part of a closet reserved for these items. It's one-stop morning shopping. I keep spare exercise clothes in there, plus sunglasses, scarves, gloves, peppermint and lemon essential oils, headphones, extra socks, herbal teas, light weights, and more. If I still had little people at home, I would keep their "morning things" in there too. I would include the departure clothing items, and I would also include a "morning box" of quiet things they could do if they were up about the same time that I was.

I truly believe that mornings are a daily gift from Heavenly Parents who love us.

POSSIBLE TASKS BEFORE BREAKFAST

Children can also have good mornings. Of course, like all of us, they can also have bad mornings. We are doing what we can. As we say in our family, "We're all just walking each other home." Sometimes I say, in comically frustrating moments, "We're all just gently kicking each other's backsides home." We are getting there.

Because children wake up hungry in the morning, it's a built-in incentive for them to get things done before that meal. Here are some basic tasks they could possibly do before breakfast: make their beds, shower, dress, do a small chore or two, bring down their laundry basket, and/or place their shoes and backpack near the door. Of course, if they are headed for school, getting all the way dressed before breakfast should be the first thing on the list. This method works wonders in keeping the stress level down as departure time gets closer.

You don't need to require major chores before breakfast, but you do want to require enough tasks to establish some routines that can bless them always. They are hungry, so they are motivated to do some simple tasks fast. They will balk as you start out with these "few extras before breakfast" requirements. Stay the course! Remember our formula: kindness plus firmness with a dose of compassion. They will likely whine but will eventually go up and get those few things done. Reward them with lavish praise and a hearty breakfast.

The Saints tend to be big fans of family prayers, and having a family prayer in the morning is a great way to launch a day. In our family, we have often had prayers and a devotional *after* breakfast when everyone is in the best possible mood.

EVENING ROUTINES

I love it when I routinely write down plans for the next day, and possibly beyond, before I go to bed each night. It feels so good to be mentally prepared for the day ahead. I also feel like when I do this, the ideas marinate in my brain overnight, and in the morning I am served up some delicious ideas about how to accomplish the tasks. I am so much more efficient and productive when I plan ahead. Even if that planning takes place in the mornings, rather than the night before, I am so much better off with a plan.

PRAYER/SERVICE LIST

In the evenings I often write down names of people who might need prayers or some sort of actionable help. My rule is that if I can do the action (send an email, a text, or a photo) in under two minutes, I try to do it right then. If I can't do it that fast, it goes on the list and calendar.

PERSONAL CARE

A part of my evening routine that I am religious about is skincare. This hearkens back to seeing my mom's bottle of Revlon's "Moon Drops" moisturizer on her dresser. She was routinely protective of her skin, and I have followed her lead. I love a hot bath with lots of add-ons. I like to add bath bombs or Epsom salts, not only for the scent but also for the magnesium they contain. Magnesium is a miracle worker in the health world. I love the book *The Magnesium Miracle*. Whatever the health issue, magnesium can likely help. Magnesium helps us to relax and get to sleep more easily as well. I also like to add baking soda to the bath for detoxification.

TIME TOGETHER

Like many families, likely including yours, we routinely try to spend time with each other in the evenings. This isn't always possible, and we have to work at it. As I type this, I have a granddaughter on one side of me and a grandson on the other. Two daughters are chatting in front of me, and one daughter is holding a third grandchild. Two teens and my husband have been rotating in and out of the room.

Sometimes Grandpa is playing with the kids. Sometimes he is working in his office. The days and evenings are never dull. But evenings have a slower, more relaxed pace that can engender deeper conversations. Often these happen as an extension of scripture/ prayer time, which also happens in the evenings.

FOOD PREPARATION ROUTINES

Meals together are a gift we can give ourselves. They take planning, but as you know, there are many resources available for planning meals. One of the best things I ever did concerning meal planning (and I wish I had done it more) was to prep dinner or at least parts of dinner while making the children breakfast in the mornings. We're already in the kitchen stirring things and opening the refrigerator. It's not a huge leap to stir some dinner things, open the refrigerator a few more times, and open a few cans. I also like to chop up vegetables on Saturdays and place them in containers in the refrigerator to eat throughout the week.

There is an oft-quoted Latter-day Saint scripture that reads, "If ye are prepared ye shall not fear" (D&C 38:30). I can't overstate how helpful that scripture is to me. I rely on it to motivate me to get things done ahead, which helps me stay calm.

One day I was sitting in an Education Week class at BYU and the teacher, author Marie Ricks, shared an idea that I have never forgotten. I am still getting around to doing it, but I hope I get there soon because it's such an excellent time-saving idea:

1. Write down a year's worth of meal ideas. You can immediately see why I haven't done this yet, but stay with me. It gets better. Basically, think about meals that you are already making, and write them down. Then throw in a handful of recipes you would like to try. Write those down.

2. Plug these meals into a calendar for a year. Of course, you will be rotating the meals. Marie suggests a two-week rotation.

3. Look at all of the ingredients for all of these meals carefully. Ask yourself which of the items can be purchased as food storage. (Latter-day Saints are fans of a reasonable amount of food storage as part of being prepared for a possible earthquake or other disaster). In other words, are there some canned or bottled items that you could possibly get a whole lot of at Costco or elsewhere? Write these items down.

4. Buckle up for this one. Purchase enough of these items to cover a year of said meals. Yes, this is a lot of canned goods to purchase at once!

How cool would it be to have fifty-two weeks of meals mostly prepped? You would only need to buy the fresh items. Please find a way to contact me and make me do this.

FAMILY COUNCILS

Family council is one of my favorite routine Latter-day Saint meetings because it sets the stage for less stress for the following week, and often beyond. We discuss what is on the calendar, what needs to be added to the calendar, goals, needs, and other family issues. Often we also plan meals for the week. This is so helpful. We figure out who is cooking which day that week and what we want to have. Because we have so many family members living close, we often access "the hood" as we divide up many of the meals.

LAUGHING/BONDING

We can laugh routinely, and we should. Nothing de-stresses like laughing with family and friends. Laughter builds the immune system. As the good book says, "A merry heart doeth good like a medicine" (Proverbs 17:22).

One day the two youngest kids, a few older ones, and I were having a teaching moment. I remember feeling emphatic as I shared the final point: "Kids, God is in the details, but if we're not careful the devil can be in the details too." No one spoke right away, as most of them were likely trying to figure out what I was talking about. I probably wasn't entirely sure either.

Then Rachel, a tween at the time, said soberly, "No, Mom, the devil is not in the details. He's in the deli." She paused as we stared at her. "Have you seen the bottoms of pre-packaged deli sandwiches? Have you seen how soggy they can be?" She rolled her eyes to the back of her head in mock horror.

Rachel is hilarious. In fact, we're deeply grateful that all of our kids inherited the goofball gene. This gene goes back to my crazy-in-a-good-way family of origin. Even though we are now adults with some adult children of our own, we do and say ridiculous things routinely.

A number of my siblings are excellent imitators. I cherish voice mails I have received from "Jimmy Stewart," "Laura Bush," "Sarah Palin," "Queen Elizabeth," "John Wayne," and others. We rarely stay serious in long conversations. Innocent humor is such a release.

Scientifically, it builds immunity. Just think, we're all preventing disease whenever we get together and laugh. I love spending time with my husband and children. I didn't always understand that "have joy in your posterity" thing when I was younger. That seemed so far away and extraneous. But I get it now. Hang in there when it's hard. There is so much indescribable joy ahead.

I've also learned that being goofy can pay off in all sorts of ways. Long ago Tom asked me to stop putting the kids to bed at night because I always wound up jumping on their beds and joking and teasing and getting them all riled up when they were supposed to be "un-riling." That routine went on for over two decades. I was able to get a lot done while he was helping the kids get to bed.

Innocent humor can connect us. It's said that the shortest distance between two people is a sense of humor. Why is innocence so underrated in society today, especially when it protects us from so much misery? An innocent childhood is just about the best gift you can give a child.

Not long ago, a number of us were gathered round the dining room table. There was beautiful music playing in the background. We were playing the board game Balderdash and laughing hard. My son was laughing so hard that tears were forming in his eyes, and later my son-in-law was laughing so hard he could barely read the words in front of him.

Laughter and tension are not compatible. Dark, adversarial feelings flee in the face of wholesome laughter. Humor breaks the tension. The Saints believe this is because the adversary does not have a wholesome sense of humor. When it's clean and funny, the adversary makes haste. By contrast, clean and funny are two things that the Spirit thrives on. Peace and good humor are complementary.

Honestly, clean, kind humor was my best weapon for dealing with the toughest parenting moments. This has been especially true during the teenage years. Good humor sends negativity running. Humor bonds us. One of life's greatest joys can be laughing with a bunch of teenagers and young adults. Even when some of us are away, we are still laughing with our kids through group text strings. You may be enjoying these as well. In addition, Zoom has made it possible for us to have large group video calls. What a blessing, in so many ways, to live on earth at this time.

Of course, life is far from all laughter and bonding. But we can reach for more of these. We can pray for more of these to run through our routines like golden threads of joy.

I believe Marvin J. Ashton's words: "When we realize that parents and family members can be more than blood relations and are in very deed friends, then we will have a glimpse of how our Heavenly Father wants us to live, not only as brothers and sisters but as very close friends."[13]

NUTS & BOLTS

- Orderly routines in our homes remind us subconsciously of the order and beauty we knew in heaven.
- Flexibility is a parental superpower. We can pray for it.
- Consider keeping a "three days out" plan on your mental radar.
- Assign yourself and each family member a laundry day. All laundry is washed, dried, and folded on this day. Post the list of assignments on the laundry room door. Enjoy your cleaner laundry room!
- Morning is the most glorious time of day. Enjoy as much of it as you can each day.
- Create a "morning closet" with all of the things you and your family could need to be able to quickly leave for a morning walk together.
- Give each child a small list of age-appropriate things to do before they can eat breakfast.
- Try "parking" yourself in a central location in your house as often as you can. Watch family members swirl around you, seeking connection.
- Consider making a list of all meals you might eat in a year. Save large swaths of time by shopping and storing the non-perishable items needed for these meals.

- Write down what you would like to accomplish the next day before you sleep each night. Pray about each item. Your brain will work on these things. Heaven will get to work on them too.

NOTES

1. Will Durrant, *The Story of Philosophy* (New York, NY: Simon & Schuster, 2012), 98.

2. Mike Murdock, *365 Wisdom Keys of Mike Murdock* (London, UK: Wisdom International, Inc., 2012), 3.

3. David Code, *Kids Pick up on Everything: How Parental Stress Is Toxic to Kids* (Scotts Valley, CA: Createspace, 2011).

4. Jenna Goudreau, "The Secret to Being a Power Woman: Wake up Early," *Forbes Magazine*, May 13, 2012. https://www.forbes.com/sites/jennagoudreau/2011/11/16/secret-being-power-woman-wake-up-early-sleep-success/.

5. Charles Bullock, *Home Words for Heart and Hearth* (United Kingdom: J. Nisbet, 1884), 141.

6. Henry David Thoreau and Jeffrey S. Cramer, *The Quotable Thoreau* (Princeton, NJ: Princeton University Press, 2011), 350.

7. Jenny (Hobby Help Staff), "30 Benefits of Walking 30 Minutes a Day," *Hobby Help*, May 31, 2020; https://hobbyhelp.com/walking/.

8. Kevan Lee, "The Best Time of Day for Creative Thinking," *Lifehacker*, March 11, 2014. https://lifehacker.com/the-best-time-of-day-to-get-ideas-according-to-science-1541494290.

9. Rhett Power, "5 Morning Rituals of Super Successful People." Inc.com. Inc., May 28, 2015; https://www.inc.com/rhett-power/5-morning-rituals-of-super-successful-people.html.

10. Charlene Laino, "Early Birds Get Better Grades," WebMD, June 9, 2008; https://www.webmd.com/sleep-disorders/news/20080609/early-birds-get-better-grades.

11. Laura Garnett, "The Scientific Reason Why Being a Morning Person Will Make You More Successful." Inc.com. Inc., October 18, 2018. https://www.inc.com/laura-garnett/the-scientific-reason-why-being-a-morning-person-will-make-you-more-successful.html.

12. Christoph Randler, "Defend Your Research: The Early Bird Really Does Get the Worm," *Harvard Business Review*, August 1, 2014. https://hbr.org/2010/07/defend-your-research-the-early-bird-really-does-get-the-worm.

13. Marvin J. Ashton, in *Conference Report*, Oct. 1969, 28–29.

Chapter Six
Building Traditions

*Family traditions counter alienation and confusion. They
help us define who we are; they provide something steady,
reliable and safe in a confusing world.[1]*
—Susan Lieberman

* * *

*Wherefore, be not weary in well-doing,
for ye are laying the foundation of a great work.
And out of small things
proceedeth that which is great.*
—D&C 64:33

***Traditions are the beautiful trimmings on the fortresses of love
we create with God.*** Traditions trim our loving homes with unity,
warmth, security, closeness, peace, and happiness. These trimmings
don't have to be expensive. A tradition is a ritual that creates happy
anticipation in all of us.

Traditions seem to happen in families, no matter what. For
example, once I was visiting with a new friend in her kitchen. One

wall was lined with shelves full of tall glass containers. One of those containers was filled with dry oatmeal. I complimented her on her lovely jars and mentioned that I loved a bowl of oatmeal for breakfast.

"I love it for a snack," my friend said.

"Sure," I said. "I guess a bowl of oatmeal would make a great, healthy snack."

"I didn't mean a bowl of oatmeal," my friend said. "I meant, like, handfuls of oatmeal. You know . . . dry." Her lips, a serious straight line, told me she wasn't kidding. "We had it as children," she continued. "My other favorite thing is burned toast." She explained. "When my sister and I were very young, it was just the two of us and our mom. She had to leave for work early, and she was always rushing to get out the door. Generally, she would burn the toast, have a few bites anyway, and leave the rest on the counter. Well, we got the leftover toast. It was just . . . you know . . . sort of a tradition, I guess."

She laughed a little awkwardly. "After school, we would come home to an empty house. We were so young. We didn't know how to make anything, really. But there were always these big bags of dry oatmeal in the pantry. We would dive into them with our tiny hands. We would eat it right out of the bag. So, that became another little tradition. Now it's all these years later, and sometimes my sister and I talk about how we both love burned toast and dry oatmeal. I guess it's just because we associate those things with home and family."

I nodded and smiled. I thought of their brave mom, trying to help her daughters even without a father at home, and how hard that must have been. I thought of the positivity of these two little girls trying to create traditions around whatever they could. And I thought about the family my husband and I were creating and how I wanted to pay better attention to both my conscious and inadvertent "traditionating." I thought about how traditions often take sacrifice.

When my husband and I were young and poor, our bishop counseled us, "Give your children experiences and memories over things."

My husband wanted to scrape together whatever extra money we had and some ski swap items so we could take our children skiing once in a while. I wanted to decorate. I didn't want to explore mountains. I wanted to explore Pottery Barn, even if it just turned out to be a barn full of pottery. Pottery was decor!

Then I thought about our bishop's counsel. I thought about how our young daughters had never once asked me why their bedspreads were not covered in English cabbage roses. I decided to lean into skiing. After all, I was really good at leaning back on my skis and falling over. I was ready to conquer a new tradition mountain.

Over the years I did do some decorating. But not one grown child has ever said anything to me like, "Mom, the woodgrain on that desk in my room—so incredible! Still makes me tear up." Rather, they have often waxed nostalgic about the love they feel for seemingly innumerable memories of time spent on and near mountains.

It needn't have been skiing. It could have been hiking or swimming or countless other good things. Traditions don't have to be expensive.

Don't be afraid of the opposition that will naturally present itself as you strive to establish traditions. Buckle up. It's coming. Sometimes it will tempt you to give up. Don't.

One day I was on my way to a ski lesson when a random woman stopped me. She encouraged me to go home and never ski again. Huh? I had never met this woman, but she was very concerned about the way I was moving through the little ski village, my skis cattywampus. I just could not get them arranged properly on my shoulder! My brow was furrowed. "You are going to accidentally hurt someone if you bump into them with those skis," she said sternly. I felt like I was getting called into the ski principal's office. I looked down.

"Do you even like skiing?" she asked. Did I like skiing? Well gosh, I had skied off and on for years, but there was no time to complicate this; I had a ski lesson in five minutes! I went straight to the truth, no preamble.

"You know, I don't think I *really* like skiing. I mean, I don't hate it, but I have skied for many years, and I'm still not very good at it," I said.

"Then why don't you go home, sit by a warm fire, and relax? Not everyone has to ski, you know," she said.

I thanked her awkwardly and excused myself. I had to go. Should I go to the lesson? Or should I go home and forget about all of it?

I thought about our family's skiing tradition. I thought of memories we had all made together. When I skied with the younger children, they were slow; I was slow. This worked! The older kids were zipping right past me with my husband. But we would all meet up in the lodge for lunch and talk and laughter and . . . I reset my skis on my shoulder (better this time) and hustled to my lesson.

I refused to throw all of this tradition away. As long as there were little ones to ski with me, I was going to try to ski. Looking back, I am incredibly grateful for our family skiing tradition. The fun and bonding has been incalculable. I thought about how making traditions sometimes took some sacrifice. I thought a little more about skiing and some other traditions we have made.

Most Saturday mornings for decades, my husband, Tom, has made pancakes. In the beginning, this drove me slightly and quietly crazy. My husband loves Bisquick. He is a fan of using this ingredient to produce a constant stream of no-frills pancakes. I am not anti-Bisquick, but I do love to cook and could think of so many other ways to make or add to pancakes.

But this was his thing. I already had so many other things with the kids. I could let this go. I reminded myself of the old cowboy adage, "Never miss a good opportunity to shut up." My husband was doing a fabulous thing: he was creating a tradition that would span generations.

One morning, with lots of little faces gathered around our pancake grill, our then five-year-old Jared said, "I know what I want to be when I grow up. A Pancake Daddy!" He picked up a pancake turner and waved it proudly. "And I already have a spatula!"

A box of Bisquick, some eggs, milk, and a little, growing family—this was the recipe for decades, and counting, of comforting tradition.

Traditions are a kind of "happier life" insurance. Or life *assurance*. We all have the power to consciously create positive traditions that can help children feel worthy of such efforts. Traditions help children feel valued and secure in a world that doesn't always make them feel valued or secure. Of course, things will sometimes go wrong despite our best efforts. But as my mom used to say, "Crisis plus time equals humor." Fun memories often include bumbling missteps we can laugh about later.

Some of our favorite traditions engender heavenly feelings. We love these feelings of warmth and peace. As we have planned traditions through the years, we have tried to choose ones that come with these feelings "built in." The following are family favorites.

FAMILY HOME EVENING/DEVOTIONAL

Family home evening[2] is a Latter-day Saint phrase. It refers to one night a week (usually a Monday night) that is reserved just for family time. This gives the family a chance to converse in a relaxed setting and learn something that can help them with their lives. It's simple. It doesn't always go as planned. But it all works out anyway, somehow.

A daughter told me recently, "Mom, I think I can speak for our whole family when I say we have so many wonderful memories of family home evenings and devotionals, the closeness they brought and continue to bring to our whole family. Thank you." My husband and I are just as thankful. We have loved these traditions.

We are glad the kids feel like they have grown up with comforting remembrances born from this adoptable, adaptable tradition. They now have memories they can finger like amulets of self-esteem during stressful times in their lives.

Like us, our children are far from perfect. But they are happy, addiction free, and healthy, and they are also strong in the "life things" like serving others, having a moral compass, and creating and maintaining strong relationships. These children are now some of our best friends.

I remembered watching a large family get up during BYU Education Week and talk about what they called "devotional." The whole family (twelve children!) took the stage. They began with a song and prayer. Then they worked on memorizing a poem together and then a scripture.

Then, they really blew me away. The children pulled out different instruments and began to play. There were violins and other string instruments. Someone was at the piano. This family orchestra thing, I instantly knew, was something we could never hope to accomplish. But the memorizing—that was interesting.

At the end of the class, the mom held up a book of poems. She explained that if a child could memorize poems, he or she would have an easier time memorizing all of the many things they would need to memorize for school. I took her at her word and headed home with great joy in my heart. We were going to enjoy devotionals! We were going to memorize inspiring things! We were going to make memories!

I envisioned a circle of us, all sitting in the living room, each taking a turn to share deep thoughts, feelings, and laughter. The problem was, our children then were so young and bouncy that it was a room full of "Tiggers." I could barely get them to sit still for a few minutes. There was no way. Or was there? A scene from SeaWorld popped into my head. What if I could replicate it with my children?

I went to the store and purchased a plethora of candy. Then I went home, gathered the kids in a circle in our living room, and made them a promise. "If you all can sit still for two minutes," I said, holding the bag of candy aloft, trying to sound brave and serious, "each of you shall receive one of these!" They stopped elbowing each other and giggling. They were riveted by gummy worms. It appeared that they actually were a little like the treat-seeking dolphins of SeaWorld. There was hope!

Our simple formula for devotionals was basically this:

- We sang an opening and closing song (in our case, it was usually spiritual, but there are lots of camping and other types of songs available).
- We said an opening and closing prayer (optional—this could just be an opportunity to express gratitude to others), and the kids took turns saying it.
- We shared a little message about something relevant to children. For example, it could be about the importance of sharing or how we could help people around us. All of these are heavenly principles that bring feelings of warmth and love.

- Topics were often reinforced with fun stories. *The Book of Virtues* was helpful. Over the years we talked about friendship skills, developing talents, how to keep a room tidy, and so on. We also talked about God. As soon as the children were old enough to share, we had them take turns sharing spiritual messages. It was delightful to watch them. I wish I had taken videos of this.

- We worked on memorizing poems. The following are some of our favorite memorized poems:

The Road Not Taken

by Robert Frost

Two roads diverged in a yellow wood,
And sorry I could not travel both
And be one traveler, long I stood
And looked down one as far as I could
To where it bent in the undergrowth;

Then took the other, as just as fair,
And having perhaps the better claim,
Because it was grassy and wanted wear;
Though as for that the passing there
Had worn them really about the same,

And both that morning equally lay
In leaves no step had trodden black.
Oh, I kept the first for another day!
Yet knowing how way leads on to way,
I doubted if I should ever come back.

I shall be telling this with a sigh
Somewhere ages and ages hence:
Two roads diverged in a wood, and I—
I took the one less traveled by,
And that has made all the difference.[3]

MARY JOANNE BELL

It Couldn't Be Done

Somebody said that it couldn't be done
But he with a chuckle replied
That maybe it couldn't
But he would be one
Who wouldn't say so till he'd tried.
So he buckled right in with the trace of a grin
On his face. If he worried he hid it.
He started to sing as he tackled the thing
That couldn't be done, and he did it!

Somebody scoffed: "Oh, you'll never do that;
At least no one ever has done it;"
But he took off his coat and he took off his hat
And the first thing we knew he'd begun it.
With a lift of his chin and a bit of a grin,
Without any doubting or quiddit,
He started to sing as he tackled the thing
That couldn't be done, and he did it.

There are thousands to tell you it cannot be done,
There are thousands to prophesy failure,
There are thousands to point out to you one by one,
The dangers that wait to assail you.
But just buckle in with a bit of a grin,
Just take off your coat and go to it;
Just start in to sing as you tackle the thing
That "cannot be done," and you'll do it.[4]

Stick to Your Task
Anonymous

Stick to your task till it sticks to you;
Beginners are many, but enders are few.
Honour, power, place, and praise
Will come, in time, to the one who stays.

Stick to your task till it sticks to you;

102

Bend at it, sweat at it, smile at it too;
For out of the bend and the sweat and the smile
Will come life's victories, after awhile.

America for Me
Henry Van Dyke

'Tis fine to see the Old World and travel up and down
Among the famous palaces and cities of renown,
To admire the crumbly castles and the statues and kings
But now I think I've had enough of antiquated things.

So it's home again, and home again, America for me!
My heart is turning home again and there I long to be,
In the land of youth and freedom, beyond the ocean bars,
Where the air is full of sunlight and the flag is full of stars.

Oh, London is a man's town, there's power in the air;
And Paris is a woman's town, with flowers in her hair;
And it's sweet to dream in Venice, and it's great to study Rome;
But when it comes to living there is no place like home.

I like the German fir-woods in green battalions drilled;
I like the gardens of Versailles with flashing fountains filled;
But, oh, to take your hand, my dear, and ramble for a day
In the friendly western woodland where Nature has her sway!

I know that Europe's wonderful, yet something seems to lack!
The Past is too much with her, and the people looking back.
But the glory of the Present is to make the Future free—
We love our land for what she is and what she is to be.

Oh, it's home again, and home again, America for me!
I want a ship that's westward bound to plough the rolling sea,
To the blessed Land of Room Enough, beyond the ocean bars,
Where the air is full of sunlight and the flag is full of stars.[5]

We remember these poems, and we will never forget feelings of love and laughter that were (and still are) in the room when we held a devotional. The bonding power has been far more significant than I would have guessed.

We have held devotional (you could easily call it "gathering time" or something else) for over two decades now. As the kids have gotten older, we let them take turns teaching devotionals and family home evenings. We have witnessed the truth of the statement, "The teacher learns the most."

A crucial part of the plan was to refrain from any criticism. There was one exception: corrections if there were reverence issues. Even here, I tried to keep it light, focusing more on rewards than consequences. Often, I would add a bonus prize for "the reverence child," the one who had exhibited the most peaceful behavior and best listening skills during the devotional.

This got comical at times as the kids began to compete with each other for the prize. They wanted to know every criterion particular. So, I added "good posture." Later, on a whim, I added "compliments for Mom." It was hilarious to see so many little squared shoulders offering things like, "You are so pretty, Mommy!" (Often I was in an "early morning" sweatshirt and sweatpants and my hair was a mess).

Especially in the beginning, I talked about the special feeling (of love and closeness) we got to enjoy when we were all together and talking about "happiness things." That feeling, I explained, was like a delicate soap bubble. A lot of bounciness could easily pop it. To feel the happiness, we had to sit still.

We eventually worked our way up from sitting still for two minutes to five minutes to twenty, and for many years now we haven't needed any treats at all. It makes me so happy that our kids in their twenties, when they are home, are happy to pop into the living room for devotionals and family home evenings. It's really pretty "Pavlovian" at this point. The kids hear "devotional" or "family night" and, with little to no prodding, they just show up and enjoy.

We still get off topic all the time and laugh and goof off, but we are together. The feeling of heavenly love that surrounds us in these times is, I believe, the best feeling on earth.

SPECIAL DATES

When our children were small, my husband was constantly über busy as a young professional, and we had little extra money for babysitters. But I wanted them to feel that special feeling you can have with a mom when it's just one on one. So, I would still take each one (in our minivan) on "special dates." It became a memorable tradition, in more ways than one.

On special dates each one got to have my attention all to themselves. The twist was that all the other children were in the van too, in the back! This made for some hilarious experiences because the special date child got to sit up front, choose all the conversational topics, and decide which fast food drive-through they wanted to patronize. No one else in the car got any choices or food at that time. I hope this doesn't sound mean. I fed them well before we left.

None of the "invisible children" (as we called them) got to order anything, but they knew that their own special turns were coming. We have very funny memories from this time, primarily because the "peanut gallery" in the back of the van would make unsolicited comments, and we would all break up laughing. Then we would try to return to "invisible children/special date child" mode, which could only last for so long before we all started laughing again. We didn't always accomplish the original goal, but we accomplished bonding goals.

READING WITH SMALL CHILDREN

Did you have a mother or father or other loved one who read to you? If you did, can you recall the incredible joy of those memories? It's a joy so sublime it's hard to articulate.

It's so many things at once: it's comforting being all snuggled up with loved ones and feeling protected, fascinating as we learn together, creative as our imaginations take flight. And it's often a time filled with naturally arising silliness and giggles. This is my personal favorite go-to tradition. I have loved it as both a child and a mother.

It should be a childhood mainstay. It is not to be missed. If you were not read to as a child, I really encourage you to go to a library and get started filling your home and children's lives with children's books. You won't regret it, and you may create some of your best memories of all, together.

As Strickland Gillian has said, "You may have tangible wealth untold, caskets of jewels and coffers of gold. But richer than I you can never be, I had a mother who read to me."[6]

Fathers reading to children, of course, is an equally delightful gift. This goes for grandparents too. I have some antique-style decorative suitcases in a little stack in my living room. They are filled with books to read to grandchildren.

We read to our children often while they were growing up. Reading is like the visual version of delicious, healthy lunches. Watching TV is like leftover Halloween candy. If a child consumes too much media, he/she will not be as interested in books. Healthy, delicious books for the win!

SINGING AROUND THE HOUSE

I grew up in a "singing house," and I knew this was a tradition I wanted to incorporate in the new family my husband and I were building. However, my husband doesn't always love to sing. He has a great voice and is down for the Christmas program hymns and the occasional "Earth, Wind, and Fire" song of a Saturday chore morning, but he is not a regular singer.

No matter! I sing often, and our children sing. The girls especially love to sing beautifully together. In the last few years, I have been asking for a Christmas program run by the kids for my Christmas gift. Everyone contributes something musical. For a couple of years our oldest son and his wife have sung Christmas songs for us that were truly sublime. Each performer, no matter their age or level of talent, melted my heart. Delighting in posterity is a real thing.

Singing lullabies to babies can be such a delight for both Mom and baby. When I became a mother, I called my mom and asked her to sing me the Irish songs she once sang to me as a baby. I wrote down the words and memorized them. Then I sang them to my own children. This has connected generations with love and has also connected me to one of our homelands: Ireland.

If you like, you could sing around the house. You could even make this a tradition. It brings such happy feelings. I grew up with singing. I sang to our children: musicals, silly songs, lots of hymns, some fun pop songs. When little ones would toddle out of their bedrooms in the mornings, all sleepy with tousled hair, I would sometimes hold my arms out and sing "Come and Get Your Love" by Redbone. Years later two of them told me they were watching the movie *Guardians of the Galaxy,* and it opened with this song. They had never heard anyone sing this song but their silly mommy before. They were shocked and giddy. It brought back some sweet childhood moments. Singing brings back memories like almost nothing else. This is one of the greatest gifts of music: its capacity to restore beautiful memories.

PLAYING LOVELY MUSIC

You can totally change the mood of your home with beautiful music. If you play lots of it when the children are young, they will likely grow to love it. One crazy thing that happened in this regard is that our oldest son listened to a lot of Mozart as a small child. My father loved Mozart, and in his honor, I played it for our young family (unbeknown to my dad) frequently. When this oldest son was four, we moved from New York City to Seattle. Somewhere in the move, I lost the Mozart music.

Fast forward to this son at twenty-something years. He called me one day and said, in effect, "Mom you won't believe the experience I am having. I was at Costco and found some classical music for a great price. I brought it home and played it. Mom, the Mozart stuff is incredible. I mean, seriously incredible, Mom! You've got to get some of this stuff!" I asked him which pieces were included. He told me. They were the exact same pieces I had played for him as a tiny baby through age four. We had never discussed the music then or since. I had just played it and then never played it again after the move.

My jaw dropped as he shared his enthusiasm.

It is said that whatever you deposit into the "bank" of a child's mind you get back twenty years later—with interest. Play that good music! It will pay off.

Every Sunday morning I turn on—you may have guessed it— the Tabernacle Choir at Temple Square. It's another great tradition. Currently I am also in a "Dan Gibson's Solitudes" phase. You can feel your blood pressure heading downward when you turn this music on.

TELLING THE TRUTH

I won't lie. This one seems odd to include as a tradition, but I can't think of a better one. Simply, truthfully explaining why we weren't on time, better prepared, interested, hurt—you name it—calms everything down. Taking responsibility and apologizing truthfully when necessary is one of the greatest gifts we can model or teach. Recently I told my husband, "I need some space." I could have left it there, but he is my closest friend. Later that night I went back and explained. "I feel like this is dumb," I said truthfully, "but I needed space because I was embarrassed. I was trying a new cooking technique, and I was burning things right and left. You were standing there, and the dish I made was getting charred and then some and . . . "

He said, "No worries at all. I don't care; I love you."

I said, "I know, and thank you. Still, I felt foolish and incompetent. My pride was goading me because I tell myself I'm a decent cook." It was so freeing to be able to just tell the truth about a pride moment. Kids have pride moments too; we all do. We can set an example for them. "I'm sorry I didn't get to the store for the thing you needed that I said I would get. I blew it." Or, "I'm sorry I wasn't as patient with you as I should have been." Whatever the situation, gentle honesty does what the Savior says it will. It sets us free; we can be imperfect. Others can be imperfect. We can all be a mess sometimes. It's okay. We are all, as they say, "just walking each other home."

MAKING BEDS

I am no domestic goddess, but I make my bed almost every single day. This makes me really happy. I read once that Nelson Mandela, even when a prisoner for years, made his bed in his tiny room every morning. What a fantastic way to start the day. Every time I walk back into my room throughout the day, my made bed gives me a zing of joy. We can help our children have this zing of joy too, even when sometimes the rest of the room doesn't follow suit.

GIVING NICKNAMES OF AFFIRMATION

Consider giving each child a positive nickname. Jesus showed us by example how powerful this can be. He called James and John "The Sons of Thunder" (how empowering would that be?). He called John "Beloved." He called Simon "Peter" because it meant "rock." All of these names helped the disciples feel their own inner strength. What wonderful nicknames could you give your children to help them too?

HAVING A FAMILY CAUSE

Having a family cause can unite everyone in a shared pursuit of goodness. We can do a run, walk, bake sale, or other event to raise money and awareness of our family cause. Do you know of someone who is experiencing a major illness? What about dedicating your family cause to this illness and person? You could Google related fundraisers and raise money together through runs or other events. Warning: Major bonding all around may ensue.

SAYING "I LOVE YOU" WITH EVERY DEPARTURE

Say, "I love you," with every departure. We never know in this uncertain world if these will be the last words. We are so comfortable with this tradition that my husband fondly recalls our son yelling, "I love you, Dad!" across a crowd of fellow teen water polo players on their way out to a game. We even say this to each other when we end a phone call.

CELEBRATING A JOYOUS DAY OF REST

Keeping the Sabbath Day holy is a refuge
from the storms of life.[7]
—Quentin L. Cook

What if we had a day that was focused on family in a calm, relationship-building, holy sort of way? We do have a day like that! It's fallen out of public fashion, but the Saints believe it's never fallen out of God's fashion. He's never taken back this command (the fourth commandment): "Remember the Sabbath Day to keep it holy. Six days you shall labor and do all your work, but the seventh day is a Sabbath to the Lord your God. On it you shall not do any work, neither you, nor your son or daughter, nor your male or female servant, nor your animals, nor any foreigner residing in your towns."

Latter-day Saints and those of many other faiths believe that one day of the week should be set aside for a day of rest. Why? This is because they believe that God has commanded them to take a day off, just as He did, after creating the world. The Sabbath day is a holy, sacred day that reminds us that we are holy, sacred beings.

If we kept this commandment all across the world, what would happen? Imagine if everyone had a day to celebrate their relationships with holiness. Imagine how much more reverent and peaceful we would be as humans.

Setting aside a sacred day of rest may be the most important family tradition of all.

NUTS & BOLTS

- Be on the prayerful lookout for positive traditions you would like to create.

- If you have devotionals on the regular, it might be your favorite tradition of all. It can engender so much relaxed fun and, often, spiritual conversation. It is my favorite tradition of all.
- Consider creating and/or maintaining the following traditions:
    - Reading with small children.
    - Having special "only child" dates.
    - Sing often around your house.
    - Make your bed, and have kids make their beds before breakfast.
    - Give children nicknames of affirmation.
    - Hold family councils.
    - Have a family game night.
    - Say, "I love you," with every departure.
    - Enjoy a Sabbath, or "rest day" once a week. This one comes with lots of potential blessings.[8]
    - Add new traditions anytime. My husband and I have a new one we just started with our grandchildren: we call them early on the morning of their birthdays and sing "Happy Birthday" to each one, together!

NOTES

1. Justin Coulson, "Family Traditions Help Kids Make Sense of Life," Institute for Family Studies, February 2, 2017. https://ifstudies.org/blog/family-traditions-help-kids-make-sense-of-life/.

2. Topics, "Family Home Evening," https://www.churchofjesuschrist.org/topics/family-home-evening?lang=eng.

3. Robert Frost, *The Road Not Taken, Birches, and Other Poems* (Claremont, CA: Claremont Canyon Press, 2010), 9.

4. Edgar Guest, and Roger Edwards, *The Little Things and Such One More Time: Motivational Poems You Know and Love Now with Reflection Questions* (Scotts Valley, CA: Createspace 2013), 16.

5. Henry Van Dyke, *The Poems of Henry Van Dyke* (United States: Scribner's Sons, 1912), 140.

6. Strickland Gillilan, "Poetry: The Reading Mother," *Owlish Books & Movies*, January 3, 2018; https://owlishbooks.com/2017/06/09/poetry-the-reading-mother-strickland-gillilan/.

7. Quentin L. Cook, "Shipshape and Bristol Fashion: Be Temple Worthy—in Good Times and Bad Times," *Ensign,* Nov. 2015, 41–42.

8. "The Blessing of Keeping the Sabbath Day Holy," *Ensign*, November 2000. https://www.churchofjesuschrist.org/study/general-conference/2000/10/the-blessing-of-keeping-the-sabbath-day-holy?lang=eng

Chapter Seven

Building Ourselves

None of us come to this earth to gain our worth;
we brought it with us.[1]
—Sheri L. Dew

* * *

Stop scouring people's faces for evidence that you're not
enough. You will always find it because you've made that
your goal. True belonging and self-worth are not goods; we
don't negotiate their value with the world. The truth about
who we are lives in our hearts.[2]
—Brené Brown

* * *

You really have to love yourself to get anything done.[3]
—Lucille Ball

Accepting God's love for us is the foundation of the stronger home we are building. Latter-day Saints believe in love: love of God, love of family, love of neighbor, and love of self. That last one can be tough to remember as we are focused on the previous three.

Years ago, I called my mom and told her I was working at a mental hospital. The patients were sweet and unpredictable. Some chased me, some wanted to snuggle, some cried hysterically. Sometimes the same people did all of these. All of them had delusions of grandeur. Some thought they were superheroes; others were royal princesses. The scene I was describing was my own home, stuffed with little children. Fun, but insane.

Time flies. Our second youngest just left for BYU—Provo, where my husband and I and all of our other children but one (still in high school) also received degrees. Six of our children are married. We have seven grandchildren and more on the way. Many of them live nearby. It's happiness, delight, and sometimes high-action toddler chaos.

As a young mom, I remember being uniquely tired sometimes. If you are a young parent, you know this all-consuming brand of tired. One day, desperate for a recharge, I planned a full day off. My husband agreed to watch all the little children (six at the time), and I would do whatever I wanted.

I had a lot planned, so I left early. I was so excited! I had a mental list of all the things: shopping, a pedicure, meals out at fun restaurants whilst reading, and more. I needed time to regroup, to think deeply. Here it was at last! As I drove away, I cranked up the radio and sang along. I drove and drove. We live about forty minutes from a major shopping area. At about the thirty-minute mark, profound exhaustion suddenly washed over me like an ocean wave. Yikes. I knew I couldn't drive like this. I pulled off the freeway and, finally, into town.

"I'll just stop, grab a bite, and hydrate. That will help, I thought. So I pulled into a fast food drive-through and ate in the car. Afterward, I instantly conked out. I was fast and deeply asleep. When I finally shook myself awake and looked at the time, four and a half hours had gone by. If you know this level of parental exhaustion, I am with you.

Even though that day (like so many days) didn't go exactly as planned, I sensed that building a stronger family involved building ever stronger editions of me. Any credit for progress I have made in this area goes to God. We can't see God now because we were sent to Earth to walk by faith, but He is here. He is watching over you. He loves you.

I would like to whisper something in your virtual ear: *You are of infinite worth.* It's true. You may already know this, but in case you didn't before, please never doubt it. Latter-day Saints and many others believe we are all children of divine heritage. We believe that God is literally the father of our spirits. Our powers and talents may not be fully developed yet, but they can be, over time. We believe that we have come to earth to try to learn to be more like our Heavenly Father (and Mother—more on this later). We may feel that we are now only the embryonic versions of our best selves. That's the way it is supposed to be. Potential takes time to achieve. Great glory is ahead.

Little by little, we get stronger. I've had to tell myself, "Buckle up, buttercup. Don't get too harried or perfectionistic about getting stronger emotionally, physically, mentally, or spiritually. Just get busy." Getting stronger starts with love for that person you have known forever, the one who looks back at you in the mirror.

When I was sixteen I asked my dad, "Do you love Mom?" I knew he did, but my teenage heart was trying to figure out nuances around the whole "love" thing.

Dad's answer took me off guard. He said, "The truth is, it depends on the day. I mean, I always love your mom. But I love her far more on the days when I love myself more, and I love her less when I love myself less." Hmm. Wasn't breathless love supposed to transcend everything? Had pop songs been lying to me? But Father knew best on this. My stronger self had to begin with loving me more. That love had to begin with understanding myself better then taking better care of myself, internally and externally. One of the most interesting, surprising things I have learned is that our bodies are actually temples, sacred places in which to house our spirits. Our spirits are who we are. Our bodies are the outside part, the temples we see. Our spirits are the part of us that never dies.

THE BODY/TEMPLE CONNECTION

The Saints believe that the human body is a gift from God of incalculable worth. Considering the body to be a temple is not an exclusively Latter-day Saint belief. Many people of faiths all over the world believe this. What a wonderful belief! In the Bible, Paul asks, "Know ye not that your body is the temple of the Holy Ghost which is in you, which ye have of God, and ye are not your own?" (1 Corinthians 6:19). Are you struck by the responsibility of this body/temple connection? I am!

One of our most important jobs on Earth is to care for our temples. When we honor them, we can better honor the temples of others. Our bodies, our temples, are truly one of God's greatest gifts. We have to take our responsibility to care for our temples seriously. We can't be casual in this area because our bodies affect our spirits, just as our spirits affect our bodies. How we treat our temples influences our happiness levels. The Saints believe that a large part of the reason we came to earth was to experience happiness and joy. So, we've got to take good care of our temples to obtain more joy.

We have a Latter-day Saint temple not too far from our home. I have been there. The workers that care for the temple do so with intentionality and focus. I've never heard one of the workers say, "Taking care of this temple is too hard. I can't do it." Instead, day after day, temple crews just give the temple what it needs. Their temple care is consistent. Through all of this consistency, a gleaming temple and lovely grounds are maintained. I want my temple to be consistently gleaming and filled with light too. This starts with internal self-care.

INTERNAL SELF-CARE

When we love a person, we accept him or her exactly as is: the lovely with the unlovely, the strong with the fearful, the true mixed in with the façade, and of course, the only way we can do it is by accepting ourselves that way.[4]
—Fred Rogers

Caring for temples internally means caring for our eternal spirits, which reside inside us. We do this, in part, by training our thoughts to move in the direction we want them to go. Ideally, we want to think positive, uplifting, and grateful thoughts.

Unfortunately, those are not always the thoughts that enter our heads. The opposite kind of thoughts tend to pop up, don't they? Latter-day Saints believe that tempting thoughts come from an actual tempter—the adversary, or devil.[5] We don't have to allow tempting thoughts to stay in our minds. Imagine your mind as a stage. When unwanted thoughts appear on your stage, remember that you are the director of your own mortal "play." We can direct negative thoughts off the stage.

Perfectionism, that sneaky little overdone, wanna-be, do-gooder, tempts us to think perfection is possible in this life. That's a bold lie. We can't be totally perfect on Earth, but we can be perfect one day, in eternity. For now, we can move slowly in the direction of ultimate goodness. Latter-day Saint scripture tells us, "Out of small things proceedeth that which is great" (D&C 64:33). Growth takes time. We need to be gentle and forgiving with ourselves, avoiding perfectionism, which strives to take all of our do-gooding to impossible extremes. Here is an example of this from my own imperfect, tempted-by-perfectionism life.

One whirlwind December day, I was out running holiday errands. I was slightly frantic, my hurried breath only occasionally deliberate as I focused on the many Christmas tasks ahead. The list was long; the time was short. But I believed in miracles.

No matter that two of our then young children were striving to put things in my cart faster than I could take them out, or that my Costco card had slipped to the bottom of my "why did I buy this" purse. I could not find my card! It was hard to find anything in the clutter convention that had become this purse. It was clearly too big. It was so big, in fact, that it had entered large tote bag territory.

I was stressed, but I was trying to remain calm, partially because Christmas songs everywhere kept telling me that this was "the most wonderful time of the year."

Maybe I was tired, but some of the songs felt a little like pressure. They were reminding me that on Christmas Day we humans should be the cheeriest, out in the snowiest, marshmallow toasting-est, party hosting-est, and chestnut roasting-est of all.

Sigh. I had never, to my recollection, seen a chestnut. I'm sure some had come and gone, but until that point, it was all stealth in the chestnut department. And roasting them? Huh?

I love Christmas songs, but some of them seemed to be writing Christmas checks for expectations that reality elves couldn't cash. The background music in every store I was in seemed to be begging me to "have a merry Christmas! Come on! Have one already! Do whatever it takes!"

I looked at my little children. Were there visions of sugar plums dancing in their heads that I had not fulfilled? Was there a recipe for sugar plums? A website? How was I going to create the perfectly trimmed Christmas of their supposed dreams? Or was this actually my dream?

I tried not to worry about ideals, attempting to just zoom in on the current deal. We wrapped, sang, trimmed, and hugged. We created, spilled, and cleaned in a loop. We put up lights. We looked at lights as we drove around. We laughed until tears sprung from our eyes, and sometimes tears just sprang from our eyes. We made mistakes. We forgave. We "family-ed." It was all tender and a little chaotic, and it was all good.

One night, the Christmas perfection gremlin came knocking again. My husband and children were asleep, and I was in the kitchen finishing up the final touches on my Yule log. Just kidding. My Yule log of yesteryear was on sabbatical that year.

Instead, I had purchased a Christmas sheet cake with little frosting reindeer and a sleigh. I stared at that cake in the semi-darkness of my kitchen. The perfection gremlin whispered, "You didn't make a homemade cake." I considered. This was true. "And you are far away from your parents and siblings. You miss them so much." Also true. "Don't you feel a little bit sorry for yourself?" I did! Was it time to throw a pity party? Suddenly I had a hankering for a spoonful of frosting reindeer.

Instead, I got up and walked to the family room. I looked at our Christmas tree. Maybe the cake was sub-par, maybe some family members were far, but there was that one star on our average, perfectly happy Christmas tree. That tree star was shiny. It seemed to be shining with love, acceptance, and hope.

I wasn't perfect in a million ways. That was okay. None of us are perfect. We were never meant to be perfect in this life. It's the adversary that whispers perfectionism garbage. It's not true. No one but Christ has ever achieved perfection in this life, and no one else ever will.

Behind every "glossy" life we may think we see, there is a freezer needing to be sorted, a laundry room in crisis, a grudge that won't budge, maybe even a secret illness. Everyone struggles.

It's the adversary that wants us to be self-obsessed with whether we are loved enough. He wants us to be caught in the quicksand of self-doubt. We only have so much energy in a day, and if he can get us to use it up on worrying about what others think of us, we can't use that energy to build and lift and serve others.

Knowing that the adversary is trying to tempt us away from a fierce and healthy self-love, do we have a catchphrase we can use when things go awry and we feel personally responsible? Instead of mentally chastising ourselves with unkind words, can we be gentle and self-forgiving? What if there was a catchphrase we could say to ourselves that encouraged self-forgiveness and put things in a better perspective?

My father had a favorite phrase that he used with his children: "Bay of Pigs." It seemed like whatever childhood or teen crisis we brought to Dad was met with the question, "Is this the Bay of Pigs?" (This was a reference to the failed attempt of the US government to remove the communist Castro regime from Cuba in 1961.) The conversations would generally go something like this:

CHILD: Dad, this thing that just happened (choose from dating, grades, health, or other common concerns) is like the *worst* thing that has ever happened to me.

DAD (interrupting): Is this the Bay of Pigs?

CHILD (first time having this particular conversation): Umm . . . the Bay of Pigs? I'm not sure?

DAD (sensing unfamiliarity with the topic): The Bay of Pigs was actually far worse than what you are now experiencing (looks directly at the child while furrowing his eyebrows) Far. Worse.

(Dad would then go on to explain the Bay of Pigs.)

Once in a while, siblings and I will still teasingly comfort each other under stress with the whispered giggle of "Bay of Pigs."

I have a mental catchphrase as well. It's "Kitty Hawk." This refers to that desolate stretch of sandy beach along the Carolinas where brothers Orville and Wilbur Wright first tried to make possible human flight. As you may recall, by today's standards of flight, it didn't go well. In fact, the plane they were trying to launch only went 120 feet.

To the outside observer, this could be construed as failure. But to God, it's just one early snapshot of the experience. If Orville and Wilbur could have zoomed out the lens and looked at the other end of the spectrum—what human flight is capable of today—they would have been astounded. What was frustrating and exhausting then is poignant and glorious now.

Welcome to life, marriage, family, and whatever you may be going through now. We are all at the relative beginning of a glorious eternity. We are often frustrated and exhausted. We all have moments (or days or months or years) where we feel like things are failing.

Orville and Wilbur understand. But when it seems like, metaphorically, we are endlessly gluing life's Popsicle sticks together to make life planes that never fly properly, I try to remember Kitty Hawk. This is only the beginning. We are getting there.

I say, "Kitty Hawk." Sometimes I say, "Bay of Pigs." Whatever we say, what we say to ourselves matters. Actions flow from thoughts. The psychologist William James said, "The greatest discovery of our generation is that human beings can alter their lives by altering their attitudes of mind. As you think, so shall you be."[6]

We can love our internal selves more by choosing loving thoughts. We can speak to ourselves with the recognition that we are of majestic worth. I love this quote about the balance between humility and confidence: "I am confident because I am a child of God, and I am humble because everyone else is too."

Is total perfection a perfect idea for the next life? Yes! Is chasing absolute perfection whilst being super hard on ourselves when we don't measure up a perfect idea? Of course not. But this is what the adversary whispers. He is banking on our inability to be self-critical and self-compassionate at the same time.

Kristen Neff, who created the "self-compassion scales" said, "I found in my research that the biggest reason people aren't more self-compassionate is that *they are afraid* they'll become self-indulgent. They believe self-criticism is what keeps them in line. Most people have gotten it wrong because our culture says being hard on yourself is the way to be."[7]

We can see through that false line of reasoning. When we talk kindly to ourselves, we gather internal strength. We can then pass on this strength to our families. They can learn by example to talk gently to themselves as well.

JEALOUSY

We can also watch out for another internal danger: the cancer of comparison. Doctors note symptoms of this disease when the patient turns green with envy. Jealousy has kept many a fantastic relationship from forming. This is a win for the adversary, who ever seeks to divide us. God seeks to unite us.

As our six daughters have gotten older and increasingly gorgeous, I was grateful that I had always been seeking to applaud them. I remembered the fear I had watching *Snow White* as a little girl. Why would that stepmother be so jealous of such a kind and gentle girl? I never wanted to grow up to be like that mean lady. Thanks for the cautionary tale, Mr. Disney. I have always tried to let my daughters know that they were lovely and have encouraged my husband to do the same.

Nothing steals peace like comparison or jealousy. It has divided people since before the invention of division. It's a tool of the adversary because he knows that when good people are united, they can bless families, neighborhoods, communities, and the world. Envy hopes to divert us from our innate, higher desire for unity. I've learned that there is a fine line between *admiration* of others and *desperation*. I want to always stay on the admiration side. Years ago, I crossed the line. I was miserable. I never want to cross it again. This occurred when I was a new-ish member of The Church of Jesus Christ of Latter-day Saints. I loved the doctrine. Personally, I believed it. I felt prepared for spiritual things. What I wasn't entirely prepared for were Latter-day Saint women.

Honestly, they were some of the kindest, most honest, spiritual, generous, and smart women I had ever had the privilege to know. They were also super busy. It didn't surprise me to learn that the symbol of Utah was Deseret, which means "honeybee." There were lots of busy meetings then buzzing for members of the lay congregations. Then there were more meetings, and after that, there were often meetings. If they could then fit them in, there might be a few extra meetings. I am exaggerating, of course. But church meetings beyond, well, church (think Mass for me) felt like a lot.

Then there was stuff: family home evening, genealogy, home and visiting teaching (now called "ministering"), casseroles to deliver, hearts to cheer, loads to lift. This was all so different from the housekeeper, groundskeeper, pool sweeper filled world that comprised so much of my youth.

Like all little girls growing up, I watched my mom carefully. For her, "busy" meant popping by a store after a day of being a good listener and friend to her children and husband. This level of effort felt infinitely doable. On the other hand, sometimes I felt there was no way I was going to be able to do all the "saintly" stuff. I thought, "Maybe I don't want to 'be in that number, When the Saints Come Marchin' In!'"

When my husband and I bought our first home in the Pacific Northwest, I was a foreigner in a personal town called Insecurity. Then my brand new Latter-day Saint friend Allie and her husband

and children moved in next door. We both had tiny children, who quickly became best friends. When I entered Allie's home, the first thing that struck me was "that feeling" I had come to know as the Holy Ghost.[8] It was peaceful, even in the chaos of babies and toddlers. It was such a sweet feeling. Even better, her home often smelled like homemade bread. My new friend was a wonderful cook.

Allie was also incredible at practically everything that you might associate with "Pioneer" Latter-day Saint culture. She could sew beautifully and did often. She could garden and bottle the produce. Name the craft, she had likely already done it. She even had a table saw for more crafts created from wood. Basically, in the time it took me to find my car keys, this woman could bathe a baby and can some jam.

By comparison, I felt like a scatter-brained version of the city mouse. Remember that children's story about the city mouse and the country mouse? I was the city mouse, freshly transplanted from New York City, from a life that was totally different. My visits to the Metropolitan Museum of Art with children in tow, my love of literature, Broadway musicals, and Royal Doulton pottery . . . who cared now? Not me. I was too busy comparing myself to the mom next door.

I was neither craft-oriented nor canning inclined. I did bake bread and would occasionally try to bust out some cool moves on a sewing machine. Unfortunately, a couple of times, I busted the sewing machine!

How, I wondered, did this pioneer-style Latter-day Saint wonder woman get so much done? What was up with all the crafts? It took a while, but eventually, it sunk in:

- There are likely millions of Latter-day Saints who don't give a fig newton about crafts. (There are also likely millions who don't give a Fig Newton about Fig Newtons.) The Latter-day Saint church has about 16.5 million members spread out all over the world. There are actually more Latter-day Saint members outside of the United States than inside the United States.[9]

- Pioneer Latter-day Saint culture has many awesome things to offer. But "culture" is not the same as doctrine. There are wonderful, diverse Latter-day Saints across all cultures.
- There are a few crafts I have learned to really enjoy.
- There were great things to be learned from my country mouse friend. I learned to love cooking and baking a lot more. I tried planting a garden. I stopped busting sewing machines. Eventually, I even learned to love to sew, not because I need to but because it was fun.

Here was the thing, feelings of inadequacy occasionally led me to feelings of jealousy. Oddly, my friend was also a bit insecure too, and this combination wasn't ideal for a beautiful friendship.

There was a lot to learn about "completing each other" versus "competing with each other." Today I sincerely value this woman and friend. I am grateful for our many fun and hilarious times together. She has taught me so much, and not just about crafts.

Life is constantly trying to teach all of us its lessons. This whole earthly experience was set up as a classroom. We learn form every single experience. One life lesson many moms learn is that "mometition" (mom+competition) can be dangerous because it can dissolve connection. We don't want that. We want connection, which is highly correlated with vibrant mental health. Connection builds unity, and pure unity is pure joy.

Admiration and mutual encouragement foster fabulous feelings of unity. United friendship engenders peace, inside and outside of our homes. Unity can also yield positive power. An example of this comes from our Utah sister suffragettes. It was Latter-day Saint women, working together in unity, that initially got the vote passed sooner than in other parts of the country.

I have been blessed with great friendships and sisterhoods in life, but I've had to fight jealousy temptations for some of them. It's been more than worth it.

Latter-day Saint prophet Ezra Taft Benson said, "Some of the greatest battles will be fought within the silent chambers of your own soul."[10] In our souls we can create harried or heavenly feelings.

We choose. The Bible says, "The kingdom of God is within you" (Luke 17:21). Could this be referring to the heaven we can create inside of us as we choose heavenly sorts of thoughts? William James, considered the father of American psychology, said, "The greatest weapon against stress is our ability to choose one thought over another."[11]

When I first met Theresa, one of my dearest friends in the world, I immediately noticed how intimidatingly sharp and "together" she was. I could feel the cancer of comparison trying to grow again. I was not, however, going to be fooled twice. I chose better thoughts than I had had with Allie. I firmly decided that I would never cross the line from admiration into desperation again. Comparison loses battles that humility, kindness, and humor can win. Old and new friendships flourish with extra doses of genuine love. Teresa is one of my dearest friends to this day.

Jealousy would like to poke its green dragon head into nearly all of our relationships. We don't have to let it. Loving friendship is one of the most powerful forces in the world. Friendship helps us feel supported so we can be more relaxed everywhere. Of course, we don't share with our friends all the things we would tell our spouses. Still, we can laugh with them, and the fun from our friendships can spill over into more fun with our family friendships at home. Good friends help us happily live, so we have more to cheerfully give.

If you would like to listen to more on this topic you can Google the episode entitled "Moms Meet Wonderful Mom Friends" on the *Moms Meet World* podcast. It's playing on all major and most minor platforms.

Years ago in a devotional, I brought in a large squash to illustrate some thoughts on jealousy. I stood near our fireplace with the squash beneath my feet. "When we have jealous feelings," I declared, "we must squash them!" Then I tried to stand, awkwardly, on the squash. That didn't work, so I just pretended to squash it with one foot. Later that week, I drove around with the squash on the dashboard of my car as a reminder for the kids, because I am a goofball.

LISTENING TO HEAVEN

Another way we can honor our internal selves is to try to listen to the still, small voice (the Holy Ghost) that is ever trying to lead us on good paths. The quiet "voice" of the Holy Ghost is something we feel more than we hear. You know you have possibly experienced interaction with the Holy Ghost when you have said, "I had a feeling that was going to happen" or "I have a feeling that I should do this good thing (fill in the blank)." If you have watched the children's movie *Frozen 2*, the "voice" that Elsa hears could be thought of as a simple, sweet representation of the Holy Ghost trying to help us.

We have our agency. We can choose to listen, or not. The Saints are big fans of receiving "personal revelation." In other words, they are seeking out this "voice" and are ever wanting (as another *Frozen 2* song says) to "do the next right thing."

Latter-day Saint prophet Joseph Smith wrote this about the workings of the Holy Ghost: "A person may profit by noticing the first intimation of the spirit of revelation; for instance, when you feel pure intelligence flowing into you, it may give you sudden strokes of ideas, so that by noticing it, you may find it fulfilled the same day or soon; . . . those things that were presented unto your minds by the Spirit of God, will come to pass; and thus by learning the Spirit of God and understanding it, you may grow into the principle of revelation, until you become perfect in Christ Jesus."[12]

Another Latter-day Saint leader noted that when your head and your heart are receiving the same impression, you know that you are receiving a personal revelation. There is a scripture that reads "Yea, behold, I will tell you in your mind and in your heart, by the Holy Ghost, which shall come upon you and which shall dwell in your heart. Now, behold, this is the spirit of revelation" (D&C 8:2–3).

Like learning to hear the call of one particular bird in a forest filled with many birds, we are on Earth trying to recognize the promptings of the Holy Ghost while traveling through this mortal journey where there are many worldly "voices." It's a challenge to grow in our ability to listen and follow the promptings of the Holy Ghost. It takes time. It's time well spent.

Listening to the still, small voice of goodness inside us will bring us safely back home to heaven at last. In the meantime, life can be noisy and confusing, in all kinds of ways. The key is to stick closely to God. I love this imagery: Imagine you are a child, traveling through a big, noisy city with your father. He explains to you that there will be many distracting sights and sounds as you travel through this city. The key, he tells you, is to keep holding his hand. He will keep you safe. He will guide you. Don't let go of his hand. Similarly, if we stay close to God, we will have a safer, guided, more peaceful journey on Earth.

God will help us know how to help our families in very specific ways. One day we will arrive home in heaven, grateful to have had our turns on Earth, and more grateful than ever for our families who journeyed with us.

EXTERNAL SELF-CARE

Take care of your body. It's the only place you have to live.[13]
—Jim Rohn

If you rest, you'll rust![14]
—Denise Austin

Since we love what we serve, we need to serve ourselves in order to love ourselves. Allowing ourselves positive, loving thoughts serves us internally. Intelligent exercise is one of the ways we can express love for ourselves externally.

The number-one, bar none, most important thing I have learned about exercise is that it's about *consistency*. I say this to myself consistently: Consistency beats capability (how well we can do an exercise) and content (what we choose to do for exercise). If all we did was "refrigerator door pulls" and "pastry lifts," and we did lots and lots of them every day, we would still have made progress. We are on our way to building a positive habit and mindset around some sort of regular movement. Of course, there are lots more exciting exercises to do!

I love and even crave exercise, but I was not a born exercise nut. I was a born non-exercise nut. Of course, when you are a kid, you don't think of riding your bike as exercise. I enjoyed bike riding and swimming and other "kid" things. Then I grew up. You know how busy it can be with tiny children. Making time to exercise was tough. Exercise just seemed like an additional hard thing. Even yoga, which doesn't have to be hard, felt hard. It felt like a stretch to even stretch myself in the direction of stretching. It would be another stretch to say that I ever spent extreme amounts of time stretching. But eventually, with dogged persistence, yoga won. Consistent yoga calms my "restless puppy" body down and ignites my energy at the same time.

Exercise is a gift that comes with the price tag of opposition. The Saints believe in "opposition in all things" (2 Nephi 2:11). They believe in an actual "adversary," the devil, who delivers temptations. In other words, they believe the adversary and his minions are trying to stop us whenever we are "heaven bent" on making good changes. The adversary tries to whisper that time spent taking great care of ourselves is selfish and self-absorbed. If he can't get us to feel guilty about doing good things for ourselves, he may tempt us at the other extreme by encouraging self-obsession. Fear and discouragement are perhaps the most commonly employed tools of the dark side to try to bring us down. I am familiar with them. Maybe you are too.

In my earliest yoga days, I would park in front of the studio but not get out of the car for a long time. I was so nervous about being able to do this new thing. Sometimes a few tears of frustration would appear as I peeked at my face in the rearview mirror. Occasionally, I wouldn't go in at all; I would just drive home. But I kept coming back, again and again. I began to attend classes consistently. Discouragement still tries to tap me on the shoulder, but now I recognize that temptation has a job to do. I also have a job to do. My job is to resist temptations. So now I get out of the car. I often slam the door triumphantly.

It's still challenging, though, to find time for any exercise when you are a young and busy parent, isn't it? This is why I have invented "social-cize!" It's simple. We all crave connection, and we find ways to interact with others. So, social-cizing is just exercising while chatting with others and getting things done in social settings. Walking with a friend is a classic example, but there are so many more ways to do this. Let's say you are chatting with a family member or friend. You can do this in yoga tree pose. Or you can do airplane pose, or you can do calf raises. The possibilities are many.

At first, your loved ones may raise eyebrows as you move into the yoga pose downward dog. Don't worry! They get used to you doing these things over time. It's fun! If you want to go next level (and I have) you can bust out some subtle yoga moves while waiting in lines at the post office, Costco, the gas station, and so on. I have been "social-cizing" for years, and I have never been called out on it. I am low key in formal settings. In public, I don't break out yoga moves like cat, cow, or camel pose. I've never done a handstand. But small moves like calf raises and even tree poses add up. Try it! Let's destigmatize exercise in public. Think of the time saved and the muscles gained.

If we are in a space with a little more time for more concentrated exercise, we may still have to pedal through a lot of choices on the way to finding exercises that work best for us. This can take a while. For a hot yoga minute, let's go back to the first day of a boot camp class I thought I might love. I was wrong. It turned out that I loved boots, and some camps, but not together.

In boot camp that morning we all chatted while waiting for Jill, our perky "drill sergeant" instructor. I was next to "Boston," a woman who had just qualified for the Boston marathon. Jill entered. We all stood at attention. "All right! Grab your heavier weights, and let's get started!" Suddenly, we were lifting. We were squatting. We were lifting while we were squatting. We were sweating. We were breathing hard. We were leaping on steps, weights in hand. We were running in place, keeping our heels up high, higher.

"So glad you have taken this time for you!" the instructor shouted over the music. This didn't make sense. Time for me? My idea of "me time" involved a little more dark chocolate than was being provided here. It also involved yoga pants, with optional yoga.

Jill interrupted my thoughts. "Let's run!" Run? She opened the door of the class and ran out. Her flock ran after her. Suddenly,

I was running too. We were running down the stairs and out of the gym. "Around the building three times!" she shouted. Eventually, we stopped for a moment at nearly vertical stairs. Then Jill ascended them. Her fans followed. I was not a fan. I was not ready for any of this. I was not ready, at that moment, for much of anything. I paused with hands on my knees, in front of some bushes framing the gym windows. Those windows revealed a glorious snack bar. I reconsidered. There was something for which I was ready, and that something was a bagel. I could see a basket of them just past the glass.

Runners began to zip past me. After the last runner, I went AWOL. I pushed through some scratchy bushes, hunkered down in front of the window, and waited. Before the first group made its way back to the gym, I emerged from the bushes, joining the fastest runner. We ran back to class. Jill looked at me, a little confused. I dabbed my hairline with a hand towel and looked off into the middle distance. Jill smiled. Had she figured it out?

I knew I needed to figure out an exercise that didn't involve boot camps or stairs. I considered going on slow runs. I had long seen runners. I had driven past them in our minivan packed with children. Those runners! Always running away from their problems and toward their goals. It was so impressive. I would notice their trendy, sweat-wicking athletic wear, their water bottles, their little fuel belts housing "runners only" kinds of snacks, their jogger strollers with happy children tucked inside.

It didn't seem possible that any of them could ever think a mundane thought while running. It had to be all *Chariots of Fire* in those noble heads, chins lifted, noses pointing to the sky. Sometimes I would look away from the runners and into the rearview mirror. There were my toddlers, strapped in their car seats, trying to poke each other in the eyes. Sometimes the baby was screaming. I could hear things spilling. I couldn't always tell exactly what was spilling or where the spills were landing. *Sigh.*

Jogging would release my stress, right? But getting started seemed too hard. Then one day, I went for a walk. I had some music and thought, "What the heck. I'll just try a little jogging." I clicked play and thought, "I wonder If I could just run to say, maybe a whole song, without stopping to walk." I did. I was surprised. There was still gas in the tank! Over weeks, I would add another song, and then another, and pretty soon I was jogging to ten songs in a row.

This felt like a miracle! I figured out the length of the average song (about three minutes). Then I figured out how many total songs I would need to complete a half-marathon. It hit me: a half-marathon was possible. My sneakers and I were about to run quietly into that daylight.

I've been running away from home, off and on, ever since. I ran two half marathons, slowly. I also love fast walking, especially with my daughters, three of whom live in our neighborhood. I love arm exercises on YouTube. (If you are just starting, arms are a great place to begin; you might already be lifting grocery bags and children. Arm exercises are basically more of the same. You might love them after a bit. I love standing ab exercises on YouTube. I love Denise Austin exercises anywhere. I will always love yoga.

Getting started with any exercise can be hard. The first half-hour I sometimes think, "I don't want to do this. Why am I doing this? Why is life so hard?" But in the last half-hour, I often think, "I don't want to leave. How can I stay longer? I love everyone! I forgive everyone!"

Being outside is especially fun. My mom used to say, "If you want to calm down fussy babies, take them outside. They feel at home there."

In nature, all of our senses are engaged. We can smell, and even taste, the crisp delicious air. We can inhale essential oils that are all around us in the plants and trees. The oils contain immunity building properties that help to ward off illness. We can also hear the cheerful, comforting sounds of birds. We can touch the texture of trees, bark, and flowers. We are surrounded by the wonder of God's creations. It's kind of enchanting.

Nearly every time I am outside, I think of this scripture: "Yea, all things which come of the earth, in the season thereof, are made for the benefit and the use of man, both to please the eye and to gladden the heart" (D&C 59:18). The Saints believe that God gave us nature as a gift. His handiwork is everywhere outside.

Wherever we choose to move, we know about the benefits of exercise: better bone density, greater energy, weight loss, better skin, better sleep, a greater ability to relax, and so on. For me, firmly deciding to get going is the hardest part. It's that first push where I have to really push. But once I've been out there, once I've been moving for a little while, it feels *so good*. I come back stronger in every way. What is that space called between opposition to our desire to exercise and putting on our sneakers? I think it's called faith.

NOURISHMENT

Another critical way of serving the external aspect of our temples is to eat and hydrate intelligently. Drinking plenty of water, eating well, and avoiding harmful substances are essential as we grow in loving ourselves.

Latter-day Saints believe that God created a nutrition plan and placed it in modern scripture. It's called the Word of Wisdom.[15] The Word of Wisdom is considered wise counsel from God to abstain from alcohol, all other non-medical drugs, and tobacco. The Saints are also counseled not to drink coffee or nonherbal tea (I adore herbal tea), and to eat plenty of seasonal fruits and vegetables. Can you imagine how healthy we would all be if everyone did this? The Word of Wisdom is replete with nuggets of, you guessed it, wisdom. It helps us to honor our temples (our bodies).

Years ago, when we lived in New York City, a police officer told us that if it wasn't for alcohol and drugs, he wouldn't have anything to do. Even if someone was never interested in any other aspect of the Latter-day Saint faith, they and their families would be incredibly blessed by following the Word of Wisdom.

When I first heard about it, I had no interest in becoming a saint. But it hit me that God might not want me to drink or smoke. So, *just in case* the Word of Wisdom was true, from that time forward, I never did those things. My husband took the same wisdom to heart as a teen, and all of our children and their spouses have as well. Obeying the Word of Wisdom has been another way to honor and love our temples, our bodies. The Word of Wisdom has kept us away from alcohol and other drug addictions. This has brought us a kind of secure joy we couldn't experience if we were under the influence of these substances. The Word of Wisdom also underscores the need to eat plenty of fruits and vegetables. These nutrients have also brought our bodies joy.

One area of health in which many people struggle, including me, is in avoiding refined sugar. There is no specific Latter-day Saint admonition to abstain from white sugar, but there is counsel to avoid *anything* that could be addictive. I have to be careful about sweets.

It's hard, isn't it? We're surrounded by temptation in today's processed world. It doesn't seem fair. Adam and Eve only had to deal with fruit. What if they had entered a more modern world? Would the story be more like this?

And it came to pass that God commanded Adam and Eve to partake of all the trees in the garden, except one. "Of the tree of junk food, thou mayest not eat."

And it came to pass that Adam and Eve noticed the cupcakes and barbecue potato chips that were growing thereon.

And lo, they beheld that the tree also grew cookies, candy bars, french fries, and personal-sized containers of ice cream. And after a time, it came to pass that they said unto themselves, "Let's have at it."

And they began to eat from the tree. And lo, they did wax chubbier and chubbier until they were so depressed that there was only one thing for it. More tree.

Isn't it interesting that the earliest recorded conversation between our Father in Heaven and His children was about food? There was such a classic parent-child exchange.

Healthy food and clean water fill the gas tanks of our cells. They give us the energy to exercise—that other critical factor for vibrant health. My favorite "health insurance" is a healthy green drink or two each day. There is a green powder that you can easily find at a health food store or on Amazon. These powdered greens are so easy. You don't even need to make a smoothie, steam broccoli, or make a salad. I like to drink this in the morning or add it to my healthy chocolate chip peanut butter balls. Greens help alkalize our bodies. When our bodies are in the more alkaline, as opposed to the acidic range (on the pH scale), we are far more disease resistant. Sugar is acidic, and sugar is everywhere. Greens help balance our internal pH. I tell the kids, "Green is the color of both wealth and health." Health is possibly the greatest wealth. It's worth continually pursuing.

My favorite way to start the day, in terms of nutrition, is to put a sweet potato in the oven when I first wake up. I turn the oven to 175 degrees and let it bake low and slow. This makes the sweet potato extra fluffy. So fluffy! After I have done lots of "morning things," this sweet tater is waiting for me. I put some golden butter and a little mineral salt on top and wow! All the cells inside me say, "Thanks!"

Lately, I have also been juicing with a cold press juicer. I found a small one on Amazon. The big ones are too daunting for me. But this small, adorable one is just right for juicing carrots, beets, apples, celery, and more. I squeeze some lemon on top of the mixture and stir. Then I add some high-quality, store-bought orange juice. This stretches the pressed juice a bit and sweetens it. It's so ridiculously good. Like the Garden of Eden in a glass, good. No wonder God placed Adam and Eve in a garden instead of, say, a dairy farm or a ranch. I'm not opposed to either of these, but garden produce is so alive. Thus, it makes us feel so alive and vibrant and energetic in such a delicious, healthy and non-addictive way. Fresh pressed juice also helps to increase our brain clarity and focus. We need more juice bars in the world.

Smoothies really are awesome too. I once saw Reese Witherspoon share her daily green smoothie recipe. Not only do green smoothies give us energy, but they also give our temples a vibrant glow. This is Reese's recipe. Apparently, she drinks it every day!

- 2 heads romaine lettuce
- 1/2 cup spinach
- 1/2 cup coconut water

- 1 whole banana
- 1 whole apple (core removed)
- 1 whole pear (core removed)
- 1 whole lemon (rind removed)
- Celery (optional)
- Almond butter (optional)

Directions

1. Roughly chop the romaine and add it to your blender with the spinach, coconut water banana, apple, pear, lemon, and the other optional ingredients if using (she uses a Vitamix).
2. Once that's all blended, divide evenly into two large glasses or water bottles.[16]

Both smoothies and juices have their place. Both can bless our stress.

GARDEN THEORY

Were there other reasons, besides nourishment, that God began the world in a garden? We can look at His goals for us to understand. Joseph Smith said, "Happiness is the object and design of our existence." With that in mind, it's easy to see why God sent His first children to a happy garden. In a garden, all of our God-given senses are joyfully engaged: we can hear the comforting sounds of nature; we can smell the sublime scents of flowers; we can touch the variable, fascinating textures of plants and rocks; we can see magnificence and God's handiwork everywhere; and of course, we can taste happiness as we enjoy the best kind of food the world can offer.

Gardens provide health-producing foods. When our health is strong, trials are less daunting. When we feel good, our mood is so much better. Garden foods give us the energy we need to pursue good deeds, and those good deeds bring us more happiness. Let's raise a glass of apple/carrot juice to that!

SWEET SUFFERING

Many garden foods can help minimize sugar cravings. This is great because sugar can cause spikes in blood sugar, which can lead to brain fog and emotional shakiness. After the spike comes the crash.

Refined sugar (not from the garden fruits and vegetables) is not the food of champions for wannabe calm moms. After parting ways with much refined sugar, I realized that sugar had been like "my old abusive boyfriend." I re-worded a Dolly Parton song, "You'll Come Again," to reflect this:

> Here you come again
> Lookin' better than a doughnut has a right to.
> And shakin' me up so, that all I really know
> is pretty soon I'm wondrin' how I came to
> dough-t you.
> All you gotta do is sport that icing,
> and there go all my defenses.
> Just leave it up to you and in a little while,
> you're messin' with my insulin
> and withdrawin' from my wallet!

I try to remind myself that a doughnut may look all golden and glazed, but he'll do me wrong. He'll steal collagen, which will age me prematurely, and add a roll to my midsection that didn't come from a dinner table. He'll leave me wired but tired. And in the end, he may also leave me with diabetes, heart disease, possibly cancer, and more. He's not worth it. *Sigh.* I loved him, but he only pretended to love me back.

Spending less time with sugar has changed me. I am able to focus more because my blood sugar isn't on a sugar-induced ADD roller-coaster ride. I am more able to enjoy the subtle flavor nuances of tremendous healthy foods that have been provided for our enjoyment and strength. I have also discovered some healthier alternative sweeteners, like monk fruit. There are also lots of *unhealthy* alternative sweeteners, like aspartame and sucralose. Doing the research on these and other artificial sweeteners is worth it. A source I really love is Trim Healthy Mama (books, website, podcast). These resources are created by two sisters who share great recipes for sugar-free treats and delicious healthy food in general.

CONCLUSION

The Saints believe that God has given us some great information and tools for taking care of our internal and external selves—our God given temples on earth. One major payoff of taking care of ourselves is that we can then care for others with the same kind of love. We can love our loved ones even better! This starts with accepting our imperfect selves, after which we can more fully accept others, with all of their imperfections. Healthy self-love balanced with healthy love for others is not only a good thing, it's a *commanded* thing.

Jesus was asked, "Master, which is the great commandment in the law? He responded, Thou shalt love the Lord thy God with all thy heart, and with all thy soul, and with all thy mind. This is the first and great commandment. And the second is like, unto it, Thou shalt love thy neighbor as thyself. On these two commandments hang all the law and the prophets" (Matthew 22:36–40).

Let's take a collective deep yoga breath and consider the "as thyself" part of "Love thy neighbor *as thyself*." The Savior is indicating that in order to love our neighbors we first need to love *ourselves*. In fact, the word *as* suggests that the amount of love we have for ourselves will be reflected in the amount of love we share with others. This critical part of the commandment is rarely discussed. Perhaps there is fear that self-love will morph into its evil twin, narcissism. This can't happen, however, if we keep the first commandment, to love God, in its natural place: first place. The order of these commandments is brilliant. God didn't create the first commandment for His own pleasure. He made it first to help us avoid the trap of unhealthy self-worship.

Healthy self-love means talking kindly to ourselves, which flows from choosing kind thoughts and taking faithful, reasonable care of our temples (the mortal bodies given us from God). I have sinned in this area. I haven't always kept the commandment to love myself enough. It's easy to fall into the trap of "I am so busy trying to care for those around me that I don't have the time to take really good care of me," or "I don't want to accidentally err on the side of self-absorption. I'll just go with some hurried self-care, be done with it, and be on to helping others."

The problem with this is that when we neglect balanced self-care, we can feel less confident, and when we feel less confident, we often have less to give. It's a very smart commandment we've been given, isn't it? When we love ourselves in reasonable, non-narcissistic, obsessive ways, we really can love others more.

NUTS & BOLTS

- Our bodies are gifts from a loving God. They are sacred temples for our spirits.
- It's not just okay to take great care of yourself, it's commanded by God. Our bodies are temples. Temples deserve the best care. So do you.
- When it comes to internal self-care, remember what Brigham Young said: "If you have a bad thought about yourself, tell it to go to hell because that is exactly where it came from."[17]
- Consider learning more about the process of receiving personal revelation.
- Learn more about Kristen Neff and her self-compassion mission.
- Consider having a catchphrase to allow yourself grace when things go wrong.
- Avoid comparing yourself to others. Compare yourself to your yesterday, last month, and last year self instead.
- "Squash" temptations to be jealous.
- Exercise fills our temples with vibrant energy. Expect opposition. The adversary doesn't want you to be happy.
- Look up the Word of Wisdom and ponder it. If it resonates as truth for you, live it.

- Consider buying a small, easy-to-clean juicer. Enjoy the joy of more energy and clarity of thought.
- Consider starting a garden, and/or eating more fresh garden produce. Food and mood are linked.
- Check out healthier alternatives for refined sugar, like monk fruit.

NOTES

1. Sheri L. Dew, https://www.goodreads.com/quotes/81398-none-of-us-come-to-this-earth-to-gain-our.

2. Brown Brené, *Braving the Wilderness: The Quest for True Belonging and the Courage to Stand Alone* (New York, NY: Random House, 2019), 158.

3. Megan Angelo, "Things We Learned from Lucille Ball," *Glamour Magazine*, August 6, 2013; https://www.glamour.com/story/lucille-ball.

4. Fred Rogers, *The World According to Mister Rogers: Important Things to Remember* (United States: Thorndike Press, 2004), 109.

5. M. Russell Ballard, et al. "Satan." The Church of Jesus Christ of Latter-day Saints. Accessed November 30, 2021. https://www.churchofjesus-christ.org/study/manual/gospel-topics/satan.

6. William James, https://www.inspirationalstories.com/quotes/t/william-james/

7. Kristin Neff, "Is It Self-Indulgent to Be Self-Compassionate?" Self Compassion. Center for Mindful Self-Compassion, February 22, 2015; https://self-compassion.org/is-it-self-indulgent-to-be-self-compassionate/.

8. "Holy Ghost," MormonWiki. Accessed November 30, 2021; https://www.mormonwiki.com/Holy_Ghost.

9. David Noyce, "LDS Church Membership Tops 16.5 Million as Convert Baptisms Rise by 6%," *The Salt Lake Tribune*, April 4, 2020. https://www.sltrib.com/religion/2020/04/04/lds-church-membership/.

10. Ezra Taft Benson, "In His Steps," BYU Speeches, Brigham Young University, August 11, 2021; https://speeches.byu.edu/talks/ezra-taft-benson/in-christs-steps/.

11. David Gelles, *Mindful Work: How Meditation Is Changing Business from the Inside Out* (United States: Houghton Mifflin Harcourt, 2015), 85.

12. Joseph Smith, *Teachings of the Prophet Joseph Smith.* Selected by Joseph Fielding Smith (Salt Lake City: Deseret Book, 1976), 151.

13. Jim C. Rohn, *Jim Rohn's Success Tips for an Exceptional Living* (N.p.: UB Tech, 2020), 24.

14. Denise Austin, *Sculpt Your Body with Balls and Bands: Shed Pounds and Get Firm in 12 Minutes a Day (With Your 3-Week Plan for Fast, Easy Weight Loss)* (United States: Rodale Books, 2004), 208.

15. Gospel Topics, "Word of Wisdom," https://www.churchofjesuschrist.org/study/manual/gospel-topics/word-of-wisdom?lang=eng

16. Seaver, Victoria. "Reese Witherspoon Drinks This Green Smoothie Every Day-Here's How to Make It." EatingWell. Meredith, May 28, 2020. https://www.eatingwell.com/article/7823948/reese-witherspoon-drinks-this-green-smoothie-every-day-heres-the-recipe/.

17. Brigham Young, https://www.goodreads.com/quotes/7595444-if-you-have-a-bad-thought-about-yourself-tell-it

Chapter Eight
Building a Marriage

Under the plan of heaven, the husband and wife walk side by side as companions, neither one ahead of the other, but a daughter of God and a son of God walking side by side.[1]
—President Gordon B. Hinckley

* * *

Mature love has a bliss not even imagined by newlyweds.[2]
—Boyd K. Packer

A marriage striving for ever-increasing selflessness is the framework of a strong home. One day as I was standing next to the dryer and our Mt. Never-rest of laundry, I could hear my young children playing. They were alternately crying and cheerfully chattering in that easy, emotion-shifting way that little children are known for.

My husband and I have twenty-six children. Not really. We have eight children. But when you are eight months pregnant with your sixth child, you have five previous young children, and you don't feel well, you might briefly feel sort of like you have twenty-six children.

"It's okay, Mommy will help you," I heard myself say patiently over and over again that morning. But who was I kidding? I felt awful. Was I getting the flu? I wasn't a lot of help. The oldest ones tried to help. I tried to help the oldest ones help.

Really, I just wanted to crawl back under the covers and wait for my mommy to come and save us all. But Mom was 3,000 miles away, on the east coast, with my sisters and brothers and dad. We had moved to the West Coast for my husband's job. He loved this job, even though it tried to strangle him periodically.

We were in one of those periods. He was down at the office, trying to wrestle the job monster—the mega load assignments, the critical deadlines—to the mat. I knew, I always knew, that if I really, really needed him, he would figure out a way to get home. He could kill the monster. Of course, like in the movies, the monster would eventually return, but he could kill it and walk away.

I needed him that day, but I wouldn't call. His immediate help was like a metaphorical fire extinguisher. I wasn't willing to break the glass. I wanted to be supportive. He was already helping us by working so hard on our behalf. I was okay, wasn't I?

I went upstairs and tried to lie down. The minute I did so, three tiny children climbed all over me, like kittens. I wanted to read and laugh with them as we so often did, but my heart wasn't in it. My concern was that everyone needed something—food, a fresh diaper, fresh clothing—and I needed to rally troops and get it all going. I gently peeled off the layers of children and got up. I spotted an overflowing hamper of laundry. I could take it to the laundry room. I was going downstairs anyway.

I hoisted it up, in advance of my burgeoning waist, and tried to head down the stairs. Calls of "Mommy!" followed me down. I was pretty shaky, trying to juggle that hamper and my girth. I was also just . . . shaky.

Then, like an apparition, there he was. My husband was standing at the bottom of the stairs. He had come home to help me. It was the middle of the day, his job was an hour away, and he had come to stay. How?

Inside, I collapsed with relief and joy. How did he know I needed him so much? I had never asked him to come. Had my voice sounded different on the phone when we spoke earlier that morning? Did that still small voice of goodness that lives inside us all whisper to him?

Whatever it was, I was so happy to see him that I couldn't speak. I just stood there, holding that enormous hamper, little children wrapped around my legs, a huge smile on my face. He took the basket. I took a nap.

Later, I silently thanked my mom, as I had done a seeming zillion times before, for teaching me what to look for in a husband. Mom had taken me aside at a young age, looked me straight in the eyes, and said soberly, "Marry someone who loves God more than he loves you." Wow. When you are young and starry-eyed and filled with infatuation and the grandiose thrill of being someone else's everything, this counsel might give you a moment's pause. Take the pause. If you aren't yet married, listen to my mom. She won't steer you wrong. It's solid framework counsel.

I think it's one of the best pieces of advice I have ever received or given. Mom knew there is a reason the first and greatest commandment is to "love God with all our heart, might, mind and strength" (Matthew 22:37). When we do that, every other relationship can fall into place.

When a spouse loves God first and foremost, that love will be reflected in behavior. He or she will try daily to be more like the Savior. Loyalty will shine. Trying to eschew impurity will be a constant. This person will keep his or her eyes on the prize of a forever family and will always strive to be loyal, faithful, true, and genuinely kind. Loving God fiercely helps us to be fierce in developing these qualities.

Of course, not all marriages are blessed by partners committed deeply to God. If we are married to someone void of the depth of this true commitment, we can still gently encourage our spouses in the direction of loving God, primarily by our examples. Additionally, if we love God first, we can more easily accept the little quirks that don't always present in the "quirky/fun" way. Sometimes they manifest in the "quirky/annoying" way.

My husband, Tom, and I are essentially the same in what we value, what we believe, and in how we want to live our lives. In terms of personality, however, we are vastly different. The phrase "opposites attract" has definitely proved true in our case.

Tom is soft-spoken. I can be soft-spoken, but beneath any subdued formality I may present, there is a much less subdued, far less formal girl. Tom is like Lassie: loyal, focused, and calm. I am more naturally like the loyal but bouncy and eager dog from Pixar's *Up*.

My parents were also opposites in many ways. My gentle mom was a great example of staying true to her own authentic and deep commitment to God, even when her husband was still catching up to his spiritual and emotional potential.

As a young child playing outside one day, I was approached by a little neighbor boy. He said, "Your dad can really sing. I heard him from his shower." What? Apparently, my father sang so loudly in our suburban neighborhood that he could be heard singing *from his shower*. He really could have been an opera singer! Dad's booming voice reflected his booming passion for life. Unfortunately, he also had a booming temper to go with it. As you know from the preface, this temper was his Achilles' heel.

Mom's temperament was the polar opposite. In our childhood, she reminded us of Snow White. It wasn't just the porcelain skin and jet-black hair. She was a gentle, Disney-esque, non-yeller. Dad was practicing to become a different Disney character: Old Yeller. We adored him for countless reasons, but his temper wasn't one of them. His doggone temper dogged him throughout his life, chewing up more than one relationship along the way.

Mom would get frustrated with Dad's temper. Sometimes he would send her flowers as an apology. Mom said that one day she wasn't buying the flowers he was "selling." She wanted behavior changes, not floral concessions. She sat on the edge of her bed, placed a wastebasket in front of her, and held the current bouquet of flowers. One by one, Mom snapped the heads off of the flowers and pitched them into the garbage.

Dad needed more practice with the language of love. It takes time to study, absorb, and practice this language. Isn't it worth that time? Love is the most powerful "voice" in the universe. The ability to express disagreement without being disagreeable is an astronomically positive quality worth developing.

Mom and Dad worked at it. They stayed together. This is mostly because Dad not only found God at a deep level later in life, but he also lost alcohol, as discussed in the preface. Of course, not every couple experiencing trouble should stay together. Addiction situations, including pornography addiction, may be good reasons to run. A toxic atmosphere can poison children. Every situation is individual. Prayer is critical.

When we are loyal, honest, forgiving, and gentle, it is easy for playfulness to follow. Silly, relaxed engagement in a secure marriage is a little bit of heaven on earth. Latter-day Saints sometimes speak of the temple as the place on earth where they can most fully feel the Spirit, and I get that. I adore the feeling I get when I walk through the doors of the temple. My heart soars because of the purity of the Spirit that is there.

There is another place where I feel this kind of soaring comfort: in the arms of my good husband as we fall asleep at night. My favorite sleeping recipe is two-part windows open, one part super cold weather (when available), one part snuggly quilt, and one part my husband beside me. This is quiet, giggle-inducing bliss. We are going on forty years of this comfort, and I am so deeply grateful. So many blessings can come from a long marriage.

Perspective is one of them. When you have been married for years, you can see potential arguments coming from a long distance, and you have long practice in avoiding them. You know your spouse so well that you can run the potential argument in your head. Cue all the facial expressions and long pauses. You can sidestep them.

If we need to address something critical but potentially controversial, we can remember that timing is everything. Sometimes we don't really need to say anything at all. Rabih Allamedine said, "You can tell how well a marriage is working by counting the bite marks on each partner's tongue."[3] I also love the cowboy saying, "Never miss a good opportunity to shut up." Sometimes we just need to wait for a better time. This can spark success.

The Saints believe the adversary wants us to fail, but we can out-maneuver him. When we are tempted to be unkind, we can STOP and do the following:

- See the situation through our spiritual eyes: what heavenly lesson might we be learning from this interaction?
- Take a minute. Don't respond right away. Breathe. As they say in yoga, "You always have your breath." Ten or twenty seconds of deep breathing can really calm us down.
- Own our own responsibility. The problem is not usually 100 percent the other person's fault. We can be sympathetic or even empathetic with how the other person may be feeling. What are their insecurities? What are their fears? I love the pop song "Stupid Deep." It's profound and helps me feel compassion for people who struggle to express themselves in optimal ways. This includes me.
- Pray. Pray constantly for help in not overreacting.

When we STOP, we are giving ourselves grace so that we can stay kind in challenging moments. We can always choose kindness when it's hard. We can do it.

One of my favorite marriage tools of all time is a simple phrase I learned from Brené Brown (author of many fantastic relationship books). The phrase is designed to be the "opener" as you share your side of the story. You simply start the conversation by saying, "The story I am telling myself . . ." or "The story I'm making up . . ."[4] This immediately takes the pressure off of the other person and creates a spirit of humility. It gives the listener an opportunity to disagree with the upcoming story, and it gives you the chance to admit you might be wrong.

In Brené's book *Rising Strong*, she offers an example of how she used this life hack with her husband one day. They were out swimming in a lake. She wanted to engage him in loving conversation, and she tried to do that. But every time she said something loving, he responded with short, unemotional, and distracted answers.

She told him that she was trying to connect with him, but he was unresponsive and that hurt her. The difference was that she did all this in a kind way by using the life hack phrase. She said, "The story I'm telling myself is either you looked at me while I was swimming and thought, 'Man, she's getting old. She can't even swim freestyle anymore,' or you saw me and thought, 'She sure doesn't rock a Speedo like she did twenty-five years ago.'"

Her husband explained that he wasn't trying to be rude or judgmental; he was scared. The night before, he had a dream in which he was with their kids on a raft when a speedboat came screaming toward them, and he had to pull all the children into the water so they wouldn't get killed by the raging vessel. He didn't even know what his wife was saying to him while they swam; he was just trying to concentrate on his swimming and make it back to the dock safely.

She then recalled that most boating accidents involve drinking. What if there actually was a dangerous boat nearby? With further discussion, they understood that Brené was stuck in a "shame story" that she wasn't fit or pretty enough for Steve, and Steve was stuck in a "shame story" that he wasn't strong or capable enough (to save them from a dangerous boat situation) for Brené.

By using the phrase "the story I'm telling myself" (or "the story I'm making up"), they were able to be vulnerable and offer kindness instead of self-defense. This phrase has blessed my husband and me so many times. It takes the defensiveness away. It has blessed our marriage, and it has helped us become even deeper friends.

This phrase, as you might have guessed, is used privately. Difficult discussions work best when we can take our spouses aside for private conversations. This protects dignity and increases the chance of positive outcomes. In our family, we ask the question, "Could I please have a private conversation with you?" with all family members old enough to talk. Private conversations are not reserved just for spouses.

THE BEST FRIENDSHIP PART OF MARRIAGE

I love a good marriage. I love the loyalty of it. I love the combination of ultimate security, playfulness, romance, and friendship that it offers. The commandment known as marriage is genius! A good marriage anchors us in our families. Good families anchor the world.

Peace on earth begins with peace at home, and peace at home begins with friendship.

The Prophet Joseph Smith taught that "friendship is one of the grand fundamental principles of Mormonism."[5] Friendship really is at the heart of every relationship, including our relationship with God. It's a critical component of marriage.

A recently published report on twenty-five years of landmark marital research finds that "the linchpin of a lasting marriage . . . is a simple concept with a profound impact: friendship."[6] If the friendship part of marriage is strong, the resultant trickle down family effect can be heartwarming.

I remember many times when Tom and I would discuss our children and how we could help them grow. Sometimes we would discuss them vis-à-vis categories. For example, how were they doing socially, physically, emotionally, and mentally? Tom was a very busy man, so once in a while I would email him a "state of our (family) union address" in the form of some notes on how I thought the kids were doing.

The children always needed something or other. After all, they were young and bumbling. At any given time there seemed to be at least one child that the other children referred to as "the focus child." The kids joked (but they were also serious) that no one wanted to be "the focus child" because it meant Mom was particularly concerned about you. It was like being under a microscope.

I recall feeling like our whole family was under a microscope when I attended a party at the home of one of my brothers on the East Coast years ago. At first, it was fun to be among little clusters of smiling, chatting people. I had just finished spreading some delicious artichoke dip on a cracker when a lady approached our group and asked a question. She pointed to a group of six young adults. "Does anyone know who those people are?"

We all turned to look. They were in their late teens and early twenties. It was clear they were relishing their time together. There was a lot of laughter. It was the kind of laughter that you could tell had gone on for years. Their dress was casual but lovely and modest. They were good-looking. They looked healthy. There were no pale, wan facades, indicating world-weariness or, worse, addiction. They vibrated with energy and joy. They also looked a lot like they were related. This made sense because they were related.

They were our children.

"Someone told me they are brothers and sisters. Is that true?" the woman asked our group. I nodded. She dramatically exclaimed, "I have never in my life seen siblings act like that. I've been watching them. They obviously adore each other. They are polite and respectful. They are complimentary of each other and hilarious! I don't think they drink or swear. Are these kids for real? I mean, I had siblings. I have kids that are siblings. They don't act like this! I have never seen a happier bunch of siblings in my life. I just don't get it. What is going on?"

"Those are some of our children," I said.

"What the heck?" she said. "How are they all such great friends? Mine fight all the time!"

Two of the other women nodded in agreement. It was a weird moment, seeing my offspring through someone else's eyes. Of course, they had had their moments with each other, but the laughter and friendship was, truthfully, the norm. Her comment made me wonder, "Are they that unusual?"

It was true that the college-age girls had chosen to be roommates at the same university (BYU), and our sons, who also attended there, all lived near each other. They chose to have many meals together. As they tried to figure out their futures and love lives, they had each other for sounding boards. Sometimes they argued, for sure. They argued over trivial things such as whose turn it was to drive the family car, who didn't return whose sweater, and more. But they always worked it out (sometimes after some teary phone calls to me). They laughed and chatted happily most all the time. They really were best friends.

The woman wanted to know what factors contributed to their lively friendships. I shrugged my shoulders and smiled. It was awkward. I felt a little overwhelmed by her reaction. I also felt guilty that I couldn't, in the moment, articulate good answers to her questions. I needed to slip away and ask myself the same questions. Why did they get along so well?

Why didn't I totally get it? I was their mother. My husband and I had spent an awful lot of time with them. I asked my husband what he thought. I thought his answer was great. He said that they had spent years and years of time together, so they were well practiced at being close friends. This was true. My husband also pointed out that they had that "ensemble thing" that groups can sometimes have. Think of the chemistry between cast members in the original *Star Wars*—Luke, Leia, Han, and all the rest. There was a magic there that was undeniable.

Why did they have that? I thought about Tom and me. We had that magic too, especially when we were alone. Maybe we were a little bit of an example in the "fun banter" department. We had also done a lot of homeschooling (not generally during high school) with almost zero TV.

Homeschooling helped them bond, but I think not having TV especially helped. This had given them many chances to chat. The rule was that you could only watch media on Friday afternoons through Saturday nights, and only if you had finished all your homework and chores. We had a lot of chores, so they got to spend time together doing chores too. They really got to know and love one another because we spent so much media-free time together.

We were glad that we had had so many children so close together. In the early years, it was beyond exhausting. Just keeping them all alive and well was tiring. But watching them that night through fresh eyes, I was reminded again that it had all been worth every minute. I was glad I had said yes to being their mom.

I dug deep for more answers. What had we done to have more love in our home? In part, the answers helped me write this book.

Our children were spiritually, physically, and emotionally healthy. They weren't all of these things at every moment. They made plenty of mistakes. They seemed to take turns being the worried over "focus child." Life is supposed to serve up challenges on the regular, and it never fails to deliver. The kids were pretty resilient, even in the face of some troubling illnesses for a few of them. They overcame them. They got stronger.

We believed in good nutrition and exercise, and we followed the Word of Wisdom. This meant drinking alcohol and smoking were not our choices. Without these addictions, they could think more clearly and laugh with true ease. The Word of Wisdom has been one of the greatest blessings of our lives. I can't express in earthly words what the value of practicing the Word of Wisdom has meant to the emotional well-being of our family. *What we put in our bodies matters to our souls.* We've never had to wait up for a child because we feared they were out drinking or taking drugs. As mentioned in an earlier chapter, I chose to obey the Word of Wisdom a few years before I joined the Church. For all I knew, it was a download from God. So, I obeyed it. It has blessed me and our family with its peace ever since. It can strengthen your family too.

You can also keep an eye out for strong Latter-day Saint kids and encourage friendships between them and your children. I remember stories about my grandmother, who said, when her kids were teens, "I never worry about Bill (her son) on the weekends. I know he is with those Mormon kids, and I know what they won't do. I know he's safe." I love this. She knew. Those Latter-day Saint kids who lived in the Washington DC area and rowed at the Potomac Boat Club also encouraged Bill to row with them in the Olympics. He did! They went to the Olympics twice and bonded as teammates and close friends. Obedience to the Word of Wisdom by these Latter-day Saint kids gave my grandmother the confidence to let my Uncle Bill have all of these experiences—a ripple effect!

Tom and I also tried to feed our kids healthy "spiritual food" through family nights and devotionals. We avoided impure media and read great literature, together and separately. This got harder in the later years when cell phones came along. Suddenly media of all sorts could be found instantly and everywhere. This makes parenting harder. Fortunately, God knew these things would be invented. He has helped us to learn ways to work with and around new technology.

The most important of these ways was to teach the kids the difference between good feelings that come from good things, and "off" feelings that warn us to turn things,—you guessed it—off! Because we raised them with high-value media and books, lesser media was less enticing than it might have been otherwise.

For example, I have a friend who is an excellent at-home chef. She is very consistent about making excellent meals for her family. She told me that she had grown up this way, with fresh gourmet food that her mother had made for her regularly. Even her school lunches were "extra." She was willing to take the time to make meals that were top drawer, because "lower drawer" food didn't taste even close to what she knew was possible. This is what we want with media. As we introduce children to high-quality media, art, dance, and theatre, lesser quality things will not be as enticing. I recall watching the 25th Anniversary Edition of *Les Miserables* as a family. Our feelings were touched to the core. We wanted more of this kind of light and goodness. We are forever seeking it.

What else did we do to try to help kids ride the inescapable ocean waves of worldliness? We taught them the Ten Commandments. I wish we had hung a list of them on the refrigerator. We taught them about repentance. We homeschooled sometimes. We taught them things from other chapters of this book.

Of course, there were toddler skirmishes. There were older-children fights. We saw these and tried to let them work out their differences between themselves as often as we could. We tried never to label a child as "the bad one." I stood firmly in the position that they *all* took turns being naughty. This was because I didn't want to fall into a pattern of labeling, and then "rescuing" the "good one" from "the bad one." No one wants permanent negative labels stamped on their behaviors. We tried to ignore the bad and lavishly praise the good whenever possible. That wasn't always possible, but we tried.

One of the most important things we indirectly taught them (through example) was that their father and I were the best of friends. We were respectful and kind to each other. Early on Tom asked me to promise that no matter what, we would never use the word *divorce*, even in a joking way. We never have. We rarely disagree in front of the children. All of this, I think, has helped them be respectful and kind to one another too.

Tom and I have tried to consistently share our best gifts and talents with one another. We have noticed that our Father in Heaven also gave talents to each of our children, as He does with all children. Individual gifts can give each child an extra special role in the family. These roles help them feel unique, and uniquely helpful.

There is a Latter-day Saint scripture that explains that each of us came to earth with (at the very least) one very special and particular gift: "For all have not every gift given unto them; for there are many gifts, and to every man is given a gift by the Spirit of God" (D&C 146:11). There are so many gifts and talents, and not all of them are obvious. The apostle Marvin J. Ashton wrote of some of these glorious gifts:

> The gift of asking; the gift of listening; the gift of hearing and using a still, small voice; the gift of being able to weep; the gift of avoiding contention; the gift of being agreeable; the gift of avoiding vain repetition; the gift of seeking that which is righteous; the gift of not passing judgment; the gift of looking to God for guidance; the gift of being a disciple; the gift of caring for others; the gift of being able to ponder; the gift of offering prayer; the gift of bearing a mighty testimony.

But I digress. I could relate to what the woman at the party had said about not witnessing siblings getting along really well. I had grown up with siblings I loved, but I didn't recall ever having this kind of total ease and comfort among all of us together. In my growing up years there had been more strain, more arguing. I think we wanted to be closer, but we just didn't know how to get there.

Tom and I had watched these kids of ours that were full of innocent fun and laughter, but I had been taking that for granted. The intense reaction of this woman woke me up, and I saw our children through her eyes.

Maybe the love Tom and I shared for one another helped them love each other too. Tom and I are the best of friends. When you are truly an excellent best friend, you don't yell; you support. You don't tear down; you build up. You keep charity in your heart. You are loyal in all circumstances.

The best friendship of marriage is even closer, of course, than any other sort of best friendship. In the Bible, God commands couples to "be of one flesh." There are a lot of emotions tied up in that flesh too. You are all blended together, so your emotions kind of sync. For example, if my husband is unhappy, especially with me, it's really hard for me to be happy.

The reverse is also true. It is really hard for my husband to be happy if I am unhappy, especially with him. Spouses complete one another and become part of one another. If my leg was suddenly broken, it would upend my life. Similarly, if this part of me that I call my husband feels broken, I have to tend him. I have to pray for him. When he is well, I am well. When he is broken, I feel broken too.

The most important key to a bright and vibrant marriage is charity. When I was growing up, I thought charity meant a place to which you sent money so kids could eat more of the foods you hated but that your mom told you starving kids would love to have.

After I joined the Church, I learned that charity is also defined as the pure love of Christ.[7] This was surprising, and beautiful. Charity is key to all successful relationships, including marriages and parenthood. Charity is a cornerstone in the ever-stronger home fortress from the world we are ever seeking to build. Passion is wonderful, and I am a passionate fan of passion in marriage. Charity can increase passion too. It's the balm of Gilead[8] in marriage.

BUMPS IN THE ROAD

One of many things I wish I had learned earlier in marriage is that there are little bumpy parts of the relationship road that are easy to avoid if you are paying attention. You know these little "pride bumps." These are tender internal areas where we may realize we are being ridiculous, but around which we still retain some unhealthy pride. Pride can be a big topic of discussion for the Saints. There is a semi-famous talk given by President Ezra Taft Benson that taught me more on the topic than anything else.[9] Pride is also a theme throughout the Book of Mormon. Who knew?

I love when my husband teases me in his gentle way, but only when we are alone. We have decades of inside jokes and flirtatious and silly expressions concerning countless things. I don't like it, though, when he teases me in front of the kids because they don't know all the nuances (marriage is so personal, and we love not sharing all the things), and they might tease me about the same idiosyncrasies too. It's not as funny to me if the teasing comes from the kids. Sound complicated? I guess it is, but the point is, I am a little protective of "me" in this area. Maybe it's a pride thing. I'm not sure, but I explained this situation to my husband. He was understanding and became more protective of me in this area too.

Similarly, I well know his "pride bumps" too and am mindful of them. If we are in a group setting and I see a "bump" up ahead in the conversation, I will try to carefully drive the conversation away from these few but tender areas.

The Saints believe that a fundamental tool for the adversary is contention. It's the tool he wants to use to rule over us. He would love to engage us in as many games of "defensiveness/guilt tennis" as possible. In this game, one person "serves" by saying something accusatory. Then the other person lobs a defensive/intentionally guilt-provoking response over the relationship net. The adversary then hopes, and tries to cheer for, a long, miserable rally of defensiveness, frustration, hurt feelings, anger, and so on. We can notice when we are being offered the adversarial "racquet." We can firmly decline the invitation. If we sense things are getting heated, we can request some time away from the topic, or we can find some part of the argument with which to agree. We can even compliment or try to change the subject. We can pray internally for wisdom.

We can also request private conversations when there is a tough discussion topic and we need time with just one person. This keeps things respectful and prevents unsolicited comments from "the peanut gallery." Private conversations can happen with other family members too. They are so ubiquitous in our family that I have in-law children jokingly ask, "When do I get my private conversation?"

LOVING LITTLE THINGS

Some little things are not bumpy at all. They are the little things we do for each other that we don't have to do. This is what gives them their poignancy and their future ability to render sudden drops of tears. Isn't it interesting that at funerals the "little things" are what people like to talk about the best?

One example of a big little thing was when Mitt Romney's father, George, used to give Mitt Romney's mother a flower *every single day* of their marriage. Since they were married for sixty-four years, that's 23,360 flowers. His wife, Lenore, found him after he had had a heart attack while working out on a treadmill at home. She had been looking for him when she realized she had not received that daily form of gentle service—her flower—that day.[10]

You can likely think of numerous examples of your own in this category. Little things add up to joy. They help us remember, as Mrs. Field's (that cookie lady from the eighties) has said, "Everyone wears an invisible sign that says, 'Make me feel important.'" Regular date nights not only rekindle that romance fire, but they validate us and help us feel important.

Striving to be our best selves everywhere, with everyone, helps with all of this. If we are kind in public but go home and yell, we are being hypocritical. I once heard someone say, "If you can get along with your family you can get along with anyone." I love that. We want to be the same kind of person with everyone, family or otherwise. If we are not consistent with our private and public behavior, we will be more likely to suffer from "imposter syndrome." Loneliness could be a by-product. The Savior said, "The truth shall make you free" (John 8:32). Isn't that interesting? He could have said, "The truth will make you rich!" or "The truth will help you be funnier at parties!" He could have said a lot of things. But He chose the word *free*. What do you think of when you hear this word? I think of relaxed, easy, at peace. The Savior is called "the Prince of Peace." He lives the truth/peace connection and wants this for us too. Being honest about who we are, and honestly trying to be truthful and vulnerable, sets us free. As Latter-day Saint business leader Stephen R. Covey has said,

> If I try to use human influence strategies and tactics of how to get other people to do what I want, to work better, to be more motivated, to like me and each other—while my character is fundamentally flawed, marked by duplicity and insincerity—then, in the long run, I cannot be successful. My duplicity will breed distrust, and everything I do—even using so-called good human relations techniques—will be perceived as manipulative.[11]

We are just happier and more effective, in marriage and everywhere, as we strive to ever align our public and private selves.

Best wishes with all of this. Remember, you are a child of God and deserving of great love. God loves and hears you. Ask Him to help. He will.)

(Disclaimer: all of the suggestions listed in this chapter might not apply if your spouse is deep into an addiction or an abusive lifestyle. If this is the case, my heart goes out to you. You may need counseling, and you may need to make some very tough decisions in the best interest of your children and yourself.)

NUTS & BOLTS

- My mom was right—marrying someone who loves God more than you is super smart.
- Enjoy the comfort and joy that marriage can bring. Comfort, joy, and trust can grow deeper over time.
- If a situation is tense, remember to STOP.

- See the situation through spiritual eyes. What could be the lesson available?
- Take a minute to breathe deeply before responding.
- Own our own responsibility. Can we see the other point of view with empathy?
- Pray continually for help.
- Use Brené Brown's phrase "the story I am telling myself" to sidestep defensiveness.
- Cultivate romance with the "little things" that are really big things.
- Be gentle with each other's "pride bumps."
- Have date nights every possible week. You can also put children to bed early and date at home. These times alone with each other rekindle romance and help you both feel valued.
- Remember that your spouse, and everyone else, wears an invisible sign that reads, "Make me feel important."
- Be loyal in all the ways, forever. The importance of loyalty cannot be overestimated. Marriage without loyalty is like life on earth without the sun. Loyalty is critical to growth.
- Make a pact to never use the word *divorce* as it pertains to the two of you.
- Consider reading these great books on marriage:
  1. *And They Were Not Ashamed* by Laura Brotherson (We give this to each child when they get married.)
  2. *The Empowered Wife* by Laura Doyle
  3. *Rock Solid Relationships* by Wendy Watson Nelson (She is the wife of current the Latter-day Saint prophet, Russell M. Nelson.)

NOTES

1. Gordon Hinckley, "Latter-day Counsel: Selections from Addresses of President Gordon B. Hinckley," *Ensign or Liahona*, March 2001, 64.

2. Boyd K. Packer, "The Plan of Happiness," *Church News*, The Church of Jesus Christ of Latter-day Saints, April 4, 2015; https://www.thechurchnews.com/archives/2015-04-04/president-boyd-k-packer-the-plan-of-happiness-34639.

3. Rabih Allamedine, https://www.wisefamousquotes.com/rabih-alameddine-quotes/you-can-tell-how-well-a-marriage-is-490151/.

4. Brené Brown, *Rising Strong: How the Ability to Reset Transforms the Way We Live, Love, Parent, and Lead* (United States: Random House Publishing Group, 2017), 19.

5. Joseph Smith in "Friendship," *New Era*, September 2009, 41; https://www.churchofjesuschrist.org/study/new-era/2009/09/friendship.

6. Megan Northrup and Stephen Duncan, "Nurturing Friendship in Marriage," Forever Families. Brigham Young University, August 13, 2020. https://foreverfamilies.byu.edu/nurturing-friendship-in-marriage.

7. Gospel Topics, "Charity," https://www.churchofjesuschrist.org/study/manual/gospel-topics/charity.

8. Boyd K. Packer, "The Balm of Gilead." The Church of Jesus Christ of Latter-day Saints, October 1977. https://www.churchofjesuschrist.org/study/general-conference/1977/10/the-balm-of-gilead.

9. Ezra Taft Benson, "Beware of Pride," *Ensign*, April 1989. https://www.churchofjesuschrist.org/study/general-conference/1989/04/beware-of-pride?lang=eng.

10. CNN, "Special Programming—Romney: Dad gave mom a rose every night," Youtube video, 1:04. August 30, 2012. https://www.youtube.com/watch?v=qk-csvXMvFw.

11. Stephen R. Covey, *The 7 Habits of Highly Effective People: Powerful Lessons in Personal Change* (New York, NY: Free Press, 2004), 21.

Chapter Nine
Building Vision

Where there is no vision the people perish.
—Proverbs 29

* * *

A role model . . . provides more than inspiration:
his/her very existence is confirmation of possibilities
one may have every reason to doubt, saying,
"Yes, someone like me can do this."[1]
—Sonia Sotomayor

The vision of what our family can become provides the roof for our strong home. Latter-day Saints are, if nothing else, visionary. After all, they believe in Joseph Smiths' First Vision,[2] which opened the heavens and ignited the restoration of the fulness of the Savior's gospel. They also believe in the Book of Mormon prophets like Lehi, who left Jerusalem because of a vision.

They believe in all ancient and current prophets of God, who are "seers" and "revelators." The current prophet, Russell M. Nelson, continually asks the Saints to seek their own personal revelation

161

regarding the "vision" God wants them to have for their own lives.

Of course, those who have designed celestial architecture, portraits that hang in famous galleries and bridges that take your breath away, are also called "visionaries." When Michelangelo was asked how he created incredible sculpture, he replied, "The sculpture is already complete within the marble block, before I start my work. It is already there, I just have to chisel away the superfluous material." Clearly, he "saw" what would be before it was ever actualized.

We, too, can be visionaries when it comes to our families. We can create heaven-inspired settings, moments, and memories. We can create goals for and with our families. It all begins with a vision. Vision is defined as "the ability to think about or plan the future with imagination or wisdom."

Some of us were not born visionaries. I understand these people. My sister recently sent me a home movie clip of me at age two. I'm sporting jammies and a blonde mop of tousled, rebellious hair on the top of my head. I am holding a large naked baby doll, and I am trying to drop it head first into the back of a baby stroller. My expression is at once confused and purposeful. Once the baby is awkwardly deposited, I move around to the front of the stroller to check on her well-being. Then I drag her out by the legs and start the process over again. I may have been without vision, and a little confused, but I so wanted to help.

This is how it is for a lot of us parents. We want to be more helpful in our families, but we may sometimes feel a little confused and visionless about how to do this. This is why I sometimes place quotes, like the ones below, where I can see them. These messages of truth inspire me to think big, to keep perspective. Taking the "long view" helps me to be more patient and loving.

These are some of my favorite visionary statements about mothers:

"Motherhood is near to divinity. It is the highest, holiest service to be assumed by mankind. It places her who honors its holy calling and service next to the angels."[3]

—J. Reuben Clark

Mothers can exert an influence unequaled by any other person in any other relationship.[4]

—D. Todd Christofferson

When the real history of mankind is fully disclosed, will it feature the echoes of gunfire or the shaping sound of lullabies? The great armistices made by military men or the peacemaking of women in homes and in neighborhoods? Will what happened in cradles and kitchens prove to be more controlling than what happened in congresses? When the surf of the centuries has made the great pyramids so much sand, the everlasting family will still be standing because it is a celestial institution, formed outside telestial time.[5]

—Neal A. Maxwell

These are great quotes, but I don't want you to feel pressured by them. Let's remind ourselves that moms can be moms *forever*. Our children will never be perfect in this life. Godliness and perfection are next life/heaven material.

Temptations toward painful perfectionism, on the other hand, are handed out like Halloween candy on earth. The world works overtime trying to chip off pieces of women's self-esteem. Can you feel it? From stress about working outside or inside the home (or both), to body-image issues, to the plague of pornography and more—the war on women is real.

Patricia Holland, author and wife of Latter-day Saint apostle Jeffrey R. Holland, said:

> If I were Satan and wanted to destroy a society, I think I would stage a full blown blitz on its women. I would keep them so distraught and distracted that they would never find the calming strength and serenity for which their sex has always been known. He has effectively done that, catching us in the crunch of trying to be superhuman instead of realistically striving to reach our individual purpose and unique God-given potential within such diversity.
>
> He tauntingly teases us that if we don't have it all—fame, fortune, families, and fun—and have it every minute all the

time, we have been short-changed; we are second class citizens in the race of life. You'd have to be deaf, dumb, and blind not to get these messages in today's world, and as a sex, we are struggling, and our society struggles. Drugs, teenage pregnancies, divorce, family violence, and suicide are some of the ever-increasing side effects of our collective life in the express lane.[6]

Women are more potentially powerful than we can imagine. This is especially true when we are united. It is also especially true in mothering, as indicated in the quotes above or in this one by Brigham Young: "The mothers are the moving instruments in the hands of Providence to guide the destinies of nations. . . . Consequently, you see at once what I wish to impress upon your mind is, that the mothers are the machinery that gives zest to the whole man, and guides the destinies and lives of men on the earth."[7]

What about women who may not be mothers? They still come with natural mothering tendencies. Women can always make a mothering difference in the lives around them. As the amazing Sheri Dew has so brilliantly asked, "Are we not all mothers?"[8]

The universality of our desire to mother particularly hit me one day when my niece Kathleen and I set out for a simple adventure. I was in my twenties, and Kathleen was about four years old. Our goal was to find an ice cream shop on a hot summer day. We laughed and sang as we roamed over rural Maryland hill and dale and hill and dale and hill and . . . Where was that ice cream shop?

I looked back at Kathleen in her car seat. She had no idea I was lost. This was before GPS and cell phones, and I didn't have a map. Eventually, we came upon what looked like an expanded version of Abe Lincoln's cabin. The signage said it was a bar. This Latter-day Saint had never been so happy to see a bar.

There were a lot of Harley Davidsons in the parking lot. Smoke filled the air as we approached the building to borrow a phone. I nudged the squeaky screen door open. There were three women there, sporting leather and tattoos. I looked down at my wispy espadrille sandals and Kathleen with her mermaid hair and her little summer dress and thought, "Please don't let me accidentally do something that might make anyone angry."

But I already had. When I looked up, my eyes met their eyes. Their eyes were narrowed in disapproval. Hard gazes shifted back and forth from me to my tiny niece. The nonverbal message was clear: "What do you think you're doing, bringing a child into a biker bar?" I agreed with them wordlessly. What was I doing? I was just desperate. I sputtered out my story. They let me use the phone. My sister directed me back.

There was a motherly, protective instinct in the eyes of those women in the bar that I will never forget. I don't know if those women had children, or even if they wanted children. But they had known and obeyed the unspoken "mother code" every woman brings with her to earth. There's a mother bear somewhere in every woman.

This is a good thing. We need to be on guard like never before. It's a tougher world for children to navigate than ever before. Armed with vision and determination, we can do whatever needs to be done.

Here are some visionary statements about fathers:

> *"Father is the noblest title a man can be given.*
> *It is more than a biological role.*
> *It signifies a patriarch, a leader, an exemplar, a confidant,*
> *a teacher, a hero, a friend, and ultimately a perfect being."*[9]
> —Robert L. Backman

> *"The sacred title of Father is shared with the Almighty"*[10]
> —Ezra Taft Benson

> *"Your responsibility as a father and a husband*
> *transcends any other interest in life"*[11]
> —Boyd K. Packer

Without good fathers anchoring their homes, families tend to wander into the storms of life and get lost at sea. We see that reflected in statistics such as these:

- Individuals from homes without fathers were 279 percent more likely to carry guns and deal drugs than peers who lived with their fathers.[12]
- Eighty-five percent of all children who show behavior disorders come from fatherless homes.[13]
- Seventy-one percent of high school dropouts come from fatherless homes.[14]
- Seventy-one percent of pregnant teens have no dad present in their life.[15]

Sadly, many dads portrayed in media today are far from ideal. The good news is that exemplary media fathers from the past are out there. Vintage episodes of *Leave it to Beaver, Father Knows Best, My Three Sons,* and *The Andy Griffith Show* are available. These are great shows with excellent fatherhood role models.

The *Trim Healthy Mama* podcast features a host named Danny who did not grow up with positive dad role models. But he is known for being an incredible dad. How did he do it? He said that he watched great dads in the media and emulated them. He filled his mind with the visions of what could be. He acted on these thoughts over and over again. He eventually became the husband and father he wanted to be, although he is still growing from "grace to grace" in his fatherhood calling.

Just as hopeful Olympians study former Olympic champions, we can study those who have successfully mastered traits we would like to have as we build our families. One of the people I studied was my mom. She wasn't a Latter-day Saint, but oh my, she was a saint in my book (and in this book).

I wish everyone could have known her, even for a few minutes. She was a tremendous role model. I have this childhood memory of my rambunctious brother hanging out of a window by his fingers. He is barely holding on. His kindergarten buddies are watching from below. There is a lot of screaming, a lot of confusion. And suddenly, there is Mom. With the steel-eyed focus of an athlete, she enters the room. A nervous gaggle of kids part to make way for her. She marches to the window, grabs my brother firmly by both arms, and yanks him in. She might as well have dusted off her hands victoriously. Mission accomplished. She talked to my brother afterward, firmly and directly, but she didn't yell.

This was far from Mary Gannon's first lifesaving parenting moment. Or her last. Not with three uber rambunctious boys. Not with a tiny daughter who loved to sneak out to visit random neighbors. Not with small children who could scale kitchen cupboards like mountain goats. But she did it.

Mom was one of two little girls in her calm Massachusetts household. Her beautiful baby sister, Helen, died of a terrible illness when she was only three. Mom remained and was loved and (perhaps extra) protected and treasured. She grew up, went to college, worked for the National Security Administration, married, and gave birth to six children in eight years. Her pampered upbringing had prepared her for life inside say, a spa. She was not as prepared to mother a half dozen children and oversee a home where the need for quick organizational skills was key. And she was married to a man who tested her *esprit de corps*.

Why didn't she yell? Maybe she just came this way, with solid patience, all the way down. Meanness didn't seem to cross her mind as an available option. She was created from fibers of kindness, I guess. I was created from fibers of kindness, lots of temptations to yell, and, thankfully, free choice. I have spent a lot of my life choosing to try to be patient like my mom. She is a great "soul model" for anyone.

When I was small, I thought she looked like Snow White with her coal-black hair, porcelain skin, and large eyes. Or maybe Jackie Kennedy. When I was about five, I saw a photo of Jackie Kennedy. Was she Mommy's sister? Or maybe the sister of Laura Petrie, that lady that was then on TV. Age lightened mom's hair, but not much dialed down the light of goodness inside her.

Our widowed grandmother (Nana) lived just a few minutes away. Nana was also astoundingly calm, as if the Dalai Lama had a mama more-Zen-than-him calm. I remember accidentally spilling a bottle of nail polish remover on her beautiful bedspread. I watched in horror as the acetone in the polish rapidly ate through the polyester in the fabric like a hungry animal. Nana's compassionate response? "We'll get another one, dear. Don't worry about it." Together Mom and Nana were gentility and gentleness.

When sibling fracas erupted, Mom would look at us, concerned and perplexed. She would say gently, "Little children love each other!" But it was almost a question. Her growing up years had been so different. Hers had been a small, quiet, well-behaved Irish Catholic Boston, Massachusetts, family.

Then we came along—all six of us, in eight years. We were Irish Catholic too, but we didn't turn out to be the convent atmosphere type. We were more the Notre Dame, adrenaline-fueled "Hail Mary pass" type. Mom said a lot of Hail Marys. She could never quite figure out how such adorable but frighteningly noisy children had tumbled into her life. She didn't always know how to handle us. I remember on a few occasions being out in public with Mom when we would go off the rails and she would look at a total stranger and ask, "Would you please reprimand them?"

Mom was devoted, but when she was desperate for a break, she would occasionally get in the car alone and take off for the library. One summer evening as Mom waved goodbye, Dad (think Fred Flinstone meets Perry Mason) leapt on the car hood, spread-eagle. "Don't leave!" he yelled. Mom waited. Dad yelled some more. How was he going to take care of six kids under eight without her? Mom waited again.

When he stopped yelling, Mom tossed her Jackie Kennedy/Laura Petrie hair and checked behind her. Then she slowly began to back up the Buick into our usually quiet suburban neighborhood. Dad slowly slid off the car. Neighbors eventually went back to their houses. Mom found a cozy spot in the library and got lost in a book.

At home, Dad quickly lost his mind. With kids hanging on his limbs, he called the library (no cell phones yet). Could they track down my mother? They could. "Mrs. Schuette, we have your husband on a line at the front desk. He says that he desperately needs to speak with you?"

Mom's lips were a thin, patient line. "He'll be all right." She went back to her book.

Mom possessed two deeply ingrained qualities that gave her internal fortitude to remain calm in nearly any circumstance. The first was a belief in the sobering power, responsibility, and needed vision that comes with motherhood. The following quote by James E. Faust had not been written yet, but she seemed to carry it somewhere inside of her: "There is no greater good in all the world than motherhood. The influence of a mother in the lives of her children is beyond calculation." [16]

The second quality was her personal innocence. Mom did not seem to crave mainstay vices of the world. Was it her relatively innocent upbringing? Whatever it was, when Mom had opportunities to walk on the wild side, she headed for the opposite side of the street. Her heart was pure.

Mom was a great role model, but she is only one of an innumerable number of men and women who can provide visions of what we want to become. These are those (both men and women) who embody the positive qualities in this quote by Margaret Nadauld:

> The world has enough women who are tough; we need women who are tender. There are enough women who are coarse; we need women who are kind. There are enough women who are rude; we need women who are refined. We have enough women of fame and fortune; we need more women of faith. We have enough greed; we need more goodness. We have enough vanity; we need more virtue. We have enough popularity; we need more purity. [17]

A MOTHER THERE

Members of The Church of Jesus Christ of Latter-day Saints believe that the ultimate father is our Heavenly Father. But they also believe He has a partner, our Mother in Heaven. She is the ultimate mother. Years ago, someone once asked me if I had ever heard that we have a Mother in Heaven. I hadn't heard of a Heavenly Mother, but the idea whispered sense. I believed in a Father in Heaven. *Could there reasonably be a father without a mother?* I had never considered this before, but logically, the answer had to be "no." Then I immediately wondered, "What is She like?" I think we can imagine that She is perfectly kind, gracious, lovely, and filled with pure and never-ending love. In short, She is heavenly.

She is the mother of our spirits. Our bodies are the "wrapping paper" for our spirits. Our spirits are the core of us. Thus, our perfect Heavenly Mother is the mother of what is most important about us. All of us have a perfect Mother in Heaven! I love the nod to her in this hymn (emphasis added):

O my Father, thou that dwellest
In the high and glorious place;
When shall I regain thy presence,
And again behold thy face?
In thy holy habitation
Did my spirit once reside?
In my *first* primeval childhood
Was I nurtured near thy side?

For a wise and glorious purpose
Thou hast placed me here on earth,
And withheld the recollection
Of my former friends and birth:
Yet oft-times a secret something
Whispered you're a stranger here;
And I felt that I had wandered
From a more exalted sphere.

I had learn'd to call thee father
Through thy spirit from on high;
But until the key of knowledge
Was restor'd, I knew not why.
In the heav'ns are parents single?
No, the thought makes reason stare;
Truth is reason—truth eternal
Tells me *I've a mother there.*

When I leave this frail existence—
When I lay this mortal by,

170

Father, mother, may I meet you
In your royal court on high?
Then, at length, when I've completed
All you sent me forth to do,
With your mutual approbation
Let me come and dwell with you.[18]

We walk by faith here, but in heaven, we witnessed Her pure and charitable example. I sensed a possible reference to our Mother in Heaven in the musical *Les Miserables*. In one scene a little girl, Cosette, finds herself alone in a brutal environment. She comforts herself with a memory that one could conjecture is of her Mother in Heaven. In her poignant, minor-key song "Castle on a Cloud" Cosette sings,

Nobody shouts or talks too loud,
Not in my castle on a cloud.
There is a lady all in white,
Holds me and sings a lullaby,
She's nice to see and she's soft to touch,
She says "Cosette, I love you very much."

Has anyone seen Heavenly Mother? The answer is yes. Abraham Canon, a member of the Quorum of the Twelve Apostles, recorded this experience:

One day the Prophet Joseph Smith asked him (Zebedee Coltrin) and Sidney Rigdon to accompany him into the woods to pray. When they had reached a secluded spot, Joseph laid down on his back and stretched out his arms. He told the brethren to lie one on each arm and then shut their eyes.

After they had prayed, he told them to open their eyes. They did so and they saw a brilliant light surrounding a pedestal that seemed to rest on the ground. They closed their eyes and again prayed. They then saw, on opening them, the Father seated upon a throne; they prayed again and on looking saw the Mother also; after praying and looking the fourth time they saw the Savior added to the group.

Brigham Young's daughter, Sister Susa Young Gates (a famous women's rights activist) insisted that in the formation of Father Abraham's individuality "our great Heavenly Mother was the greater molder:" greater than his genetics, his prenatal impressions, his cultural or natural environment, or even his earthly mother's nurturing. Gates speculated that Heavenly Mother has played a significant role in all our lives, looking over us with "watchful care" and providing "careful training.[19]

The 1995 "The Family: A Proclamation to the World"[20] affirms that in the eternal realms above we were reared to premortal maturity through the tutelage of heavenly parents. President Harold B. Lee stated, "We forget that we have a Heavenly Father and a Heavenly Mother who are even more concerned, probably, than our earthly father and mother, and that influences from beyond are constantly working to try to help us when we do all we can."[21] I am so glad to hear this. I need all the help I can get!

NUTS & BOLTS

- Keep an eye out for soul models. Pray for more to come into your life.
- Listen to my *Moms Meet World* podcast episode "Moms Meet Moms," where my guests and I discuss soul models.
- Learn from the examples of historical and fictional soul models.
- Post visionary parenting quotes where you can see them.

Here are some suggestions for "Mom soul models":

- Our Heavenly Mother
- Mary, the mother of our Savior
- Esther (Old Testament)
- Elizabeth (New Testament)
- Margaret March ("Marmee") from *Little Women*
- Molly Weasley from *Harry Potter*
- Caroline Ingalls from *Little House on the Prairie*
- Olive Osmond from the singing Osmond family

- Jackie Kennedy Onassis (She tried hard to be a good mother.)
- Lady Diana (She also tried hard to be a good mother.)
- Elastagirl from *The Incredibles* (That flexibility power was intentional. Moms need massive flexibility powers.)
- Sheri Dew (Her talk "Are We Not All Mothers?" is on YouTube.)
- June Cleaver from the 1960s show *Leave it To Beaver*

Here are some suggestions for "Dad soul models":

- Atticus Finch from *To Kill a Mockingbird*
- Bob Cratchit from *A Christmas Carol*
- Arthur Weasley from *Harry Potter*
- Ward Cleaver from *Leave It to Beaver*
- Stephen Keaton from *Family Ties*
- Steven Douglas from *My Three Sons*
- Andy Griffith from *The Andy Griffith Show*
- Jim Anderson from *Father Knows Best*

NOTES

1. Sonia Sotomayor, *My Beloved World* (New York, NY: Vintage Books, 2014), 227.

2. Gospel Topics, "First Vision, https://www.churchofjesuschrist.org/study/manual/gospel-topics/first-vision?lang=eng.

3. J. Reuben Clark, *Messages of the First Presidency of The Church of Jesus Christ of Latter-day Saints,* 6 vols. (1965–75), 6:178.

4. Todd D. Christofferson, "The Moral Force of Women," *Ensign* or *Liahona*, November 2013, 29.

5. Neal A. Maxwell, "The Women of God," The Church of Jesus Christ of Latter-day Saints, April 1978. https://www.churchofjesuschrist.org/study/general-conference/1978/04/the-women-of-god.

6. Patricia T. Holland, "'One Thing Needful': Becoming Women of Greater Faith in Christ," October 1987; https://www.churchofjesuschrist.org/study/ensign/1987/10/one-thing-needful-becoming-women-of-greater-faith-in-christ.

7. Brigham Young, *Discourses of Brigham Young.* Compiled by John A. Widtsoe (Salt Lake City: Deseret Book, 1954), 199–200.

8. Sheri L. Dew, "Are We Not All Mothers," *Ensign*, November 2001, 96.

9. Robert L. Backman, "What the Lord Requires of Fathers," *Ensign*, September 1989; https://www.churchofjesuschrist.org/study/ensign/1981/09/what-the-lord-requires-of-fathers?lang=eng.

10. Ezra Taft Benson, "Great Things Required of Their Fathers," The Church of Jesus Christ of Latter-day Saints, 2008; https://www.churchofjesuschrist.org/study/general-conference/1981/04/great-things-required-of-their-fathers.

11. Boyd K. Packer, "The Father and the Family," The Church of Jesus Christ of Latter-day Saints, 2008; https://www.churchofjesuschrist.org/study/general-conference/1994/04/the-father-and-the-family.

12. Clare Morell, "Fathers Matter," *National Review*, June 20, 2021. https://www.nationalreview.com/2021/06/fathers-matter/.

13. Editorial Team, "Statistics," The Fatherless Generation, April 28, 2010. https://thefatherlessgeneration.wordpress.com/statistics/.

14. Ibid.

15. Editorial Team, "Research and Statistics," Rochester Area Fatherhood Network, 1993. http://www.rochesterareafatherhoodnetwork.org/statistics.

16. James E. Faust, "Fathers, Mothers, Marriage," *Ensign or Liahona*, August 2004, 3.

17. Margaret D. Nadauld, "The Joy of Womanhood," *Ensign or Liahona*, Nov. 2000, 15.

18. "O My Father," *Hymns*, no. 292.

19. Danielle B. Wagner and Katie Lambert, "11 Powerful Truths about Our Heavenly Mother from Prophets and Apostles," *LDS Living*, September 20, 2021. https://www.ldsliving.com/11-powerful-truths-about-our-heavenly-mother-from-prophets-and-apostles/s/85272.

20. "The Family: A Proclamation to the World," *Ensign*, November 2010, 129.

21. Harold B. Lee, "The Influence and Responsibility of Women," *Relief Society Magazine* 51, no. 2 (February 1964): 85.

• LDS church callings: https://www.churchofjesuschrist.org/study/manual/general-handbook/30-callings-in-the-church?lang=eng

• Helping Hands: https://www.churchofjesuschrist.org/topics/humanitarian-service/helping-hands?lang=eng

• LDS Charities: https://www.latterdaysaintcharities.org/

• The natural man (LDS): https://www.churchofjesuschrist.org/study/scriptures/gs/natural-man?lang=eng

Chapter Ten
Building Heaven

Perhaps our life in a loving premortal world
set up our yearning for true, lasting love
here on earth. We are designed to give love
and be loved, and the deepest love comes
when we are one with God.[1]
—Neil Marriott

* * *

Nothing is going to startle us more when we
pass through the veil to the other side
than to realize how well we know our Father
and how familiar His face is to us".[2]
—Ezra Taft Benson

Our premortal home in heaven provides the ultimate blueprint for our loving earthly home. One of my best friends, Mary Pat, once owned an exquisite boutique. It was a "Monet at the seaside" feel. Soft whites. Muted greens. Lush plants, handcrafted furniture, and gentle, breezy paintings. Even the air had a hint of light perfume. It had such a relaxing effect on me.

She could see how entranced I was when I first entered her shop one day. "Mary," she said. "Do you know why we are drawn to beautiful things?" I raised my eyebrows. "It's because *we came from heaven*. Heaven was our first home. Everything there was beautiful and orderly. When we see things like that here, we feel joy and peace. We feel that we have come home."

Mary Pat is a Latter-day Saint. She was referring to our belief in a premortal existence. This is a powerful belief because behaviors, including parenting behaviors, often spring from core beliefs, values, understandings, and perspectives. An even "gently considered" Latter-day Saint outlook on life before Earth lends a perspective that can increase respect for our children. This makes parenting easier.

More specifically, Latter-day Saints believe that our children were our peers in heaven. On earth we have come into our divine family roles, arriving, as we all do, as babies. We believe that a "veil" of forgetfulness is placed between individuals and their former lives in heaven so that they can walk by faith here. This is true for all of us. Our children were valiant and brilliant then. So were we.

More on this to come, but for now let's move to another, soon-to-be-relevant beginning—a scene from my childhood. When I was about four years old, I visited Glen Echo, a theme park in Maryland, with my father and two of my brothers. I was so tiny. I was placed inside a little cart that followed a track that wound around a small theatrical scene depicting the story of Snow White.

I didn't yet know this story, and I was enchanted by the first scene of a princess in a cheerful forest of chirping birds and lovely trees. I was so happy! My toddler heart swelled with joy, and I imagine that I clapped my hands with delight. The cart jerked forward a little, and we were on to the next scene. There was another tall tree, and everything appeared, at first, to be as wonderful as before. But then I noticed that the princess was missing. And then, slowly, out from behind a tree, a witch appeared.

I still remember my utter surprise. What was a witch doing there? I thought she was scary, and I remember thinking something like, "Scary feelings are ruining all my good feelings." This was not what I wanted. I wanted those happier *heavenly* feelings back.

Latter-day Saints believe that heavenly feelings exist because we used to actually live in heaven. We can only reference heaven as a comparative point because, at a subconscious level, we already know what heaven is. Now we are on earth. Sometimes, we may feel like strangers.

In heaven, our spirits were good—even angelic, as you might imagine based on locale. If we could turn back time, lift the veil, and see our premortal selves in all their glory, we might be tempted to bow down with respect.

Our spirits are the truest part of ourselves. Our bodies make up the other part, but our mortal bodies were then just coming attractions. Now our bodies are the temples that house our spirits.

We left heaven because we wanted to receive bodies. We wanted to learn and to grow and progress here on earth. Just as earthly children want to grow to become like their earthly parents, we wanted to become more like our heavenly parents.

Have you seen the movie *Random Harvest*? This might be a "random" question, given that this film came out in 1942, but esteemed scholar Truman Madsen believes that it contains a "harvest" of interesting ideas that metaphorically parallel the concept of premortality.

The story is about a man who becomes injured in the war and suffers from amnesia. He no longer remembers that he once was the son of a good and wealthy nobleman. His life had been comfortable and happy. Now he feels alone, dazed, and confused. He is not sure who he is. Through a series of fortunate events, his full memory is at last restored to him.

Here is the parallel: We also came from a happy and comfortable home in heaven. We arrived on earth with no clear former memory of our premortal life. Eventually, we will return to heaven. All of our memories of former glory and peace will be restored.

Essentially, we are in the midst of a metaphorical three-act play. The first act is our premortality, our lives in heaven before we came here. The second act is this life, mortality. The third act is the next life.

Origen (an early Christian scholar), the Greeks, and Islam have all taught about the existence of premortality. Plato said that we are "born with knowledge from a previous life that is subdued at birth and must be relearned." He believed that we are never learning anything new. We are instead *remembering* what we already knew in our premortal realm. Plato also taught that the world we lived in before this one was perfect.³ There, we knew everything.

This concept is especially intriguing to me. I once read a true story about a man who thought he was sort of terrible at math growing up and a pretty average student in general. But one night he was robbed and struck violently in the back of the head. The injury changed his brain. Suddenly he could solve math equations with the best of them. He fell in love with math, seeing math in nature and objects all around him. He was soon considered a math genius.⁴ Isn't that fascinating? The math was already inside him. Plato would say that all knowledge is already inside of us. We came with it. But most of it is currently dormant.

In the Bible we witness the Lord referencing premortality when He says, "Before I formed thee in the belly I knew thee" (Jeremiah 1:5). There are more references to premortality that originate in ancient Jewish thought, as well as in ancient Mesopotamia and, as we have seen above with Plato, in Greece. We find extensive thinking on premortality among European and even Russian philosophers.⁵ In the nineteenth century, there were references to it in Edward (brother of Charles) Beecher's book *The Conflict of Ages: or, the Great Debate on the Moral Relations of God and Man.*

Some of my favorite thoughts on this are from Marcel Proust, a French novelist. Does this statement of his resonate with you? "Everything in our life happens as though we entered upon it with a load of obligations contracted in a previous existence . . . obligations whose sanction is not of this present life, [which] seem to belong to a different world, founded on kindness, scruples, sacrifice, a world entirely different from this one, a world whence we emerge to be born on this earth, before returning thither."⁶

Another reference to premortality in American culture is found in the movie *The Bluebird* with Shirley Temple. This film uses outdated technology, of course, so the presentation is cheesy by current standards. Still, the message is intriguing. Shirley's character visits with her sister before her sister is born. She also visits with premortal Abraham Lincoln, Queen Victoria, and Thomas Edison.

Young children sometimes have memories of life before this one. A story is told of a three-year-old girl who saw her brand new baby sister for the first time. She leaned down into the bassinet and said quietly, "Please remind me about heaven. I have almost forgotten now."

William Wordsworth penned these words about our immortal home:

> Our birth is but a sleep and a forgetting:
> The soul that rises with us our life's Star,
>
> Hath had elsewhere its setting,
> And cometh from afar:
>
> Not in entire forgetfulness,
> And not in utter nakedness,
>
> But trailing clouds of glory do we come,
> From God, who is our home.[7]

Latter-day Saints believe that a "veil" is placed between us and our heavenly memories so that we can learn to walk by faith. *New York Times* bestselling author Richard Eyre describes this veil as acting as a semi-permeable membrane. Sometimes small "truth particles" get through. Often when we are touched beyond understanding through music or literature that strongly resonates, or even a "deja vu" experience, we are connecting with these "truth particles." In his book, *Life Before Life,* Mr. Eyre states, "Within you is a spirit that lived before your physical birth and that will continue to live after your physical death. Eternity goes both ways. You lived—not as another person but as yourself—in a spiritual pre-life."[8]

Because that veil of forgetfulness was intentionally placed between us and our recollections of our heavenly home, sometimes we have a vague feeling of malaise, and we're not sure why. Latter-day Saints might attribute this to "heavenly homesickness." We experience this at a less than conscious level.

One day our then three-year-old Emily was staring up at a large painting of Jesus hanging in our stairwell. As I passed, she pleaded, "Please take that picture down!" I was confused. It was a great painting. I kneeled down and looked her right in the eyes. "Why do you want me to take it down, sweet girl?" I was now holding her gently by the hand. "Because I miss Him so much," she said. Tiny tears began to stream down her little face.

We all know the feeling of being touched by a particularly beautiful song, witnessing an especially powerful sunset, or being on the receiving end of deep and surprising kindness. Why are these experiences so memorable? Do these things remind us of heaven? Do we, at a subconscious level, miss that home? Latter-day Saints believe the answer is yes.

It was hard to leave heaven, even though we "shouted for joy!"[9] This is why we are so drawn to things that remind us of that realm. We might say things such as, "This food tastes like heaven!" or "The views on this vacation are heavenly!" We couldn't logically make that comparison to heaven if we had never been there.

When something reminds us of perfection, we are likely to associate it with that perfection we once knew. This is true in homes as well. When we are in a home that has some heavenly "design elements," we are subconsciously reminded from whence we came. We desire to recreate heaven in our own homes.

When someone dies, we often say they have "gone home." As Pierre Teilhard de Chardin has said, "We are not human beings having spiritual experiences. We are spiritual beings having human experiences."[10]

This truth may lead us to questions such as, why are little girls so often drawn to all things "princess"? Why are little boys drawn to superheroes? In the deepest part of ourselves, do they—do we—recognize our own connection as children of a heavenly king and queen?

Of course, the adversary would love it if no one ever had the slightest inkling about any of this, about our former home of great love where we were valiant and strong. Once in a while, the Spirit may gently whisper truth on the matter.

I remember a day when our oldest son was in the fourth grade. He was one of many children by then. It had been a particularly rough go with this son lately. He was so difficult that day (or was I just difficult and projecting?) that I called my husband at work and asked him to come home.

I had never done this before and, of course, he couldn't bow out that quickly. But I hung up the phone and had an idea. Maybe I could channel some of the desperate energy I was feeling into some sort of desperate prayer. I kneeled down and began speaking out loud to our Father in Heaven.

Before I even got through pleading, I felt an impression. For a very real moment in my mind's eye, I could see my young son in the premortal world. This was both surprising and comforting. He was his adult self, and I could feel kindness emanating from him. I realized that we were all glorious before we arrived on this fallen earth. He was too. I could sense his valiance. This was a micro-glimpse of his infinite worth.

I needed to figure this out. It wasn't all him. Maybe I needed to model more patience for this child, even when he wasn't patient. From then on, if he said something unkind, I decided that I would not lecture. He already knew right from wrong on this topic. I would either ignore it or say, authentically and intentionally without guile, "Please talk kindly."

At first, nothing changed. Maybe he was even worse, to test me. But after a while, I could tell he felt guilty. His behavior slowly adjusted to my keep up with my determined-to-be-kind pace. Joy increased in our home.

It would be dishonest to say we never again had a bit of a power play, but it would be honest to say that these instances were extremely rare. Today he is an adult, and we are the joint owners of a friendship that is both deep and delightful. It's built on mutual respect, and the foundation is cement strong. I have not forgotten his inherent worth, nor the reminder from heaven that we have all arrived on earth with eternal worth. Today he is a young doctor married to a lovely woman, and they have a wonderful family.

Recently at a shower for their new baby, two different women I had never before met took me aside privately. They each wanted to share with me what impact our son had had on their lives and the lives of their families. "He is a true gentleman. He has blessed our family," one of them said with a hint of emotion in her eyes. Were the years of patience worth it? You know the answer. They will be worth it for you too.

Latter-day Saints not only believe that families were critical before this life, but they believe families will also be critical after this life. No Latter-day Saint marriage ceremony ever says, "Till death do you part." The Saints believe that families are forever.

The "man upstairs" (God) is a family man. He wants families to be all "snuggled in" in this life, all trying hard to be kind and good. He wants us to build powerful bonds through sacrifice and time together. We are building for eternity. We can make our homes fortresses of faith, towers of tenderness, castles of kindness. Families are ordained of God. President Spencer W. Kimball said, "Family life is the best method for achieving happiness in this world, and it is a clear pattern given to us from the Lord about what is to be in the next world."[11]

One day we will take all that we have learned on earth back to heaven. Like a child returning from college, perhaps a little wide-eyed at the advantages he had once taken for granted at home, so we too will look at heaven with more gratitude than ever before. We will more fully realize then that we spent our lives searching for and admiring heavenly things. This is because what we were ever searching for was home.

We see this played out metaphorically in *The Wizard of Oz*. Dorthy is desperate to leave kind people in a kind place and strike out on her own. After she gets experience in the world and meets some wickedness, she has a much greater appreciation for the glimmers of heaven she left behind at home.

As T. S. Eliot said in words both poetic and profound,

> We shall not cease from exploration
> And the end of all our exploring
> Will be to arrive where we started
> And know the place for the first time
> Through the unknown, remembered gate.[12]

The more we can construct even the smallest elements of heaven into our homes, the happier and stronger our homes will be. Heaven truly is ever the blueprint for heaven in our earthly homes.

HEADING HOME

I mentioned previously that Latter-day Saints believe that there is a "veil" that separates us from our heavenly home. But sometimes, we may have experiences that involve a peek through that veil. This happened to me. I am sharing it now in conclusion to this book. We have come full circle from the preface, where you learned about the challenges of my conversion.

After my dad passed away, he came to me in a dream. I say dream, but it was so real that it felt more like somewhere between a dream and reality. This experience from "beyond the veil" woke me up, and I was filled with wonder. Afterward, I had to wake up my husband to share the experience.

In this dream, Dad and I were standing outside the home that I lived in when I was a young child. But I was an adult, dressed for running, and my father was also dressed for running. My father had never been a runner. He was a walker. But here, he ran.

We ran up the street. When we came to the top, Dad looked at me to know which way to go next. I looked back at him, unsure. I expected him to choose. But he didn't. We didn't need words to communicate. Somehow, he just indicated that he didn't know which way to go, but he knew I would know.

I chose to turn right, even though the only road was on the left-hand side of the street. We turned right. Suddenly, a vista opened up before us. It was a beautiful view, filled with sunlight and mountains. We were in Utah.

We ran down a path, side by side. It led down to the campus of BYU. We were entering the campus from just above the administration building, and not far from the "Tree of Life" statue. I was amazed. I had spent countless hours in this spot on campus as I pondered what God would like me to do with my life.

Together Dad and I beheld BYU. We both felt the glory of it. We were both happy, united, and grateful for our father-daughter friendship. The Spirit was incredibly strong. That was the end of the dream, but as it was happening, the Spirit impressed upon me its meaning.

The dream was a message about two things:

1. My dad wanted me to know that he understood where and how I had received my deep testimony of the restored gospel. BYU is so spirit-filled, it has often taken my spiritual breath away. I've spent time at a number of other colleges and universities. I have never been on a campus that filled me with the gentle, loving peace of the spirit of God like BYU. It was everywhere when I went to school there. It still is. I couldn't deny it. I also could not deny the truthfulness of the Book of Mormon. BYU was where I read that book and obtained a testimony of it.

2. My father wanted me to know that he had accepted the gospel. We ran together in unity, in symbolic recognition of our now united faith. Dad wanted me to know that he loved the gospel. He wanted me to know that he was sorry that he hadn't seen the truth of the gospel clearly in mortality.

He wanted me to know that now he understood not only the gospel but also the depth of pain I had experienced in accepting it, knowing that it would mean the breaking of our relationship for a time. He wanted me to know that he deeply understood my conversion story. He really wanted me to feel "seen." I did. Our spirits and thoughts were communicating without either of us ever having to say a word. We didn't have to—we just knew. We both understood that it was the gospel of Jesus Christ that had rebuilt our relationship, our friendship, and our partnership in doing good in the world. He was "on the other side." But he was still doing good in the world.

He wanted me to know that he loved me. I love him right back. Of course, this experience brought me great joy. Our relationship had been remodeled, updated, and ready for eternity.

Making our homes as strong as they can possibly be is worth all the labor. Of course, there will be times when metaphorical floorboards come loose, when trimmings need to be repainted, when roofs need to be repaired. Families are always a work in progress. But there is no greater work on earth.

You now have a plethora of tools and construction elements to build your stronger home. You also have the enthusiastic support of our whole family. Let's all keep building until we pass through the veil into heaven. I hear there are mansions there built by the Savior. See you there!

Let not your heart be troubled;
you believe in God, believe also in Me.
In My Father's house are many mansions;
if it were not so, I would have told you.
I go to prepare a place for you.
And if I go and prepare a place for you,
I will come again and receive you to Myself; t
hat where I am, there you may be also.
—John 14:1

NUTS & BOLTS

- Notice the next time you, or someone else, comments on the "heavenliness" of something. How can we know something is heavenly if we never knew heaven?
- Look for heavenly qualities in your family members, in your home, and in yourself.
- Keep in mind the truth about your children's identity as sons and daughters of God. You are a child of God too.
- Always know that you are truly, deeply, and eternally loved.

NOTES

1. Neill F. Marriott, "Abiding in God and Repairing the Breach," *Ensign or Liahona*, November 2017, 10.

2. Ezra Taft Benson, "Jesus Christ-Gifts and Expectations," BYU Speeches. Brigham Young University, October 15, 2021; https://speeches.byu.edu/talks/ezra-taft-benson/jesus-christ-gifts-expectations/.

3. Wikipedia Contributors, "Pre-Existence." Wikipedia. Wikipedia Foundation, October 12, 2021; https://en.wikipedia.org/wiki/Pre-existence.

4. Sarah Keating, "The Violent Attack That Turned a Man into a Maths Genius." BBC Future. BBC, July 8, 2020; https://www.bbc.com/future/article/20190411-the-violent-attack-that-turned-a-man-into-a-maths-genius.

5. Terryl Givens, *When Souls Had Wings Pre-Mortal Existence in Western Thought* (Oxford, UK: Oxford University Press), 2012.

6. Marcel Proust, in Gabriel Marcel, *Homo Viator,* (1963), 8.

7. William Wordsworth, "Ode: Intimations of Immortality from . . ." Poetry Foundation, *Poetry Magazine,* 2021. https://www.poetryfoundation.org/poems/45536/ode-intimations-of-immortality-from-recollections-of-early-childhood.

8. Richard M. Eyre, *Life before Life: Origins of the Soul—Knowing Where You Came from and Who You Really Are* (Salt Lake City, UT: Shadow Mountain, 2000).

9. Guide to the Scriptures, "Premortal Life," https://www.churchofjesuschrist.org/study/scriptures/gs/premortal-life?lang=eng.

10. Wayne W. Dyer, *You'll See It When You Believe It: The Way to Your Personal Transformation* (New York, NY: William Morrow, 1989), 16.

11. Spencer W. Kimball, "Privileges and Responsibilities of Sisters," *Ensign or Liahona,* Nov. 1978, 103.

12. T. S. Eliot, *Four Quartets* (Boston, MA: Houghton Mifflin Harcourt Trade & Reference Publishers, 1968), 49.

About the Author

MaryJo Bell is a graduate of BYU, the mother of eight children, and the grandmother of eight more. She is the host of the popular podcast *Moms Meet World*. She has written for *The Huffington Post*, *Thrive Global*, *Segullah*, and *Real Clear Religion*. She currently writes a monthly column for *Meridian Magazine*. MaryJo has appeared on KSL's *Studio 5* program, discussing "Nanahood."

MaryJo loves to smile/laugh in every possible situation with family and friends, especially while singing, cooking, and thinking about future (currently nonexistent) exciting gardening skills.